OPPORTUNITIES

in

Social Work Careers

W9-BVE-484

OPPORTUNITIES

in

Social Work
Careers

REVISED EDITION

RENEE WITTENBERG

VGM Career Books

Chicago   New York   San Francisco   Lisbon   London   Madrid   Mexico City
Milan   New Delhi   San Juan   Seoul   Singapore   Sydney   Toronto

The *McGraw·Hill* Companies

Library of Congress Cataloging-in-Publication Data

Wittenberg, Renee.
   Opportunities in social work careers / Renee Wittenberg.—Rev. ed.
      p. cm.—(VGM opportunities series)
      ISBN 0-07-139049-9 (paperback)
      1. Social service—United States.   2. Social service—Canada.   3. Social
   service—Vocational guidance—United States.   4. Social service—Vocational
   guidance—Canada.   I. Title.   II. Series.

   HV91 .W56   2002
   361′.0023′73—dc21   2002069025

1 2 3 4 5 6 7 8 9 0   LBM/LBM   1 0 9 8 7 6 5 4 3 2

ISBN 0-07-139049-9

McGraw-Hill books are available at special quantity discounts to use as premiums and
sales promotions, or for use in corporate training programs. For more information,
please write to the Director of Special Sales, Professional Publishing, McGraw-Hill, Two
Penn Plaza, New York, NY 10121-2298. Or contact your local bookstore.

This book is printed on acid-free paper.

Contents

Foreword   ix

Introduction   xi

1. **Historical Trends in Social Work**   1

    Religious background. Industrial Revolution. Charity
    Organization Society. Medical social work. Social
    casework. Settlements. Educational influences. Social
    Security Act. Social work and social welfare. Civil
    rights. School social work. Paraprofessionals. Clinical
    social work. Schools of social work. Public assistance.
    Social services. Trends for services.

2. **Social Work Qualifications**   23

    Professional levels/degrees. Personal abilities.
    Registration versus licensure. Private practice/clinical
    social work. Other resources. State qualifications.

3. Areas of Social Work 41

Family and child welfare services. Aging and elderly
services. Mental health facilities. Medical settings.
Corrections. School social work. Community
organization. Industrial social work. Private practice.

4. Jobs in the Profession 67

Child welfare caseworker. Family counselor or family
caseworker. Social service caseworker. Case aide or
eligibility worker. Casework supervisor. Social welfare
administrator/director. Psychiatric social worker.
Clinical social worker, private practice. Medical/hospital
social worker. School social worker. Industrial social
worker. Social group worker. Program aide in group
work. Tenant relations coordinator. Community
organization worker. Parole officer. Probation officer.

5. Prospects in the Social Work Field 87

The shifting family structure. Medical waivers.
Deinstitutionalization. Case management. Homeless
population. Acquired Immune Deficiency Syndrome
(AIDS). Child abuse. Networking. Personal values
and beliefs. Professional overlapping. Job outlook.
Earnings. Career advancement. Licensing. Working
conditions. Additional social concerns.

6. Setting Personal Goals 105

Evaluating career goals. Narrowing your choices.
Education. Financial aid. Your decision.

7. Locating a Job 117

Job skills and job duties. The résumé. State and
federal government positions. Additional job leads.
The interview.

8. Social Work Opportunities in Canada 127

Canadian Association of Schools of Social Work.
Education and training. Canadian Association of
Social Workers. Certification/registration.

9. Related Occupations 135

Psychologists. Counselors. Social and human service
assistants. Clergy.

Appendix A: National Associations and
   Organizations 147
Appendix B: Canadian Associations 153
Appendix C: Journals 157
Appendix D: Further Reading 163
Glossary 167

Foreword

IF YOU WOULD enjoy working on behalf of others, especially those disadvantaged by poverty and oppression, a career in social work may be right for you.

Social work is a profession committed to two broad goals: assisting and empowering individuals to overcome problems in their daily lives, and improving social and economic conditions for all vulnerable populations. These two goals require professionals who have skills and knowledge in human behavior, social interaction, community organization, social policy, and research methods.

Social work professionals practice in many settings and with many different populations. For example, social workers serve as clinicians and case managers in child and family welfare agencies, mental health clinics, substance abuse programs, public schools, and hospitals; as administrators of social service programs; as community organizers; and as social welfare policy analysts and lobbyists. Because the situations they confront are complex—helping troubled families, strengthening communities, working with individuals who face multiple problems—social workers often work closely with other "helping professionals" such as teachers, doctors, nurses, psychologists, and clergy.

Those interested in the social work profession usually begin acquiring the needed knowledge and skills as undergraduates. In the United States today, approximately forty-five thousand students are enrolled in some 420 baccalaureate social work programs accredited by the Council on Social Work Education (CSWE). Individuals who go on to graduate school generally focus their studies on specific populations or settings. About thirty-eight thousand students are enrolled in 140 CSWE-accredited master of social work degree programs in the United States.

People choose a career in social work for a variety of reasons, but one common motivation is to make a real difference in the lives of those in need. Social work can be tremendously challenging and rewarding to those who make this commitment. To decide if you are suited to a career in social work, please read about and consider the opportunities described in this book.

Donald W. Beless
Executive Director
Council on Social Work Education

Introduction

Social workers are people who are specially trained to provide counseling, support, and guidance to people in need. Their help allows people to understand themselves and their living conditions and to attain their full potential. Social workers also try to improve living conditions by becoming involved in programs that deal with such social problems as poverty, alcoholism, drug abuse, behavior problems, child abuse, mental illness, crime, housing, and physical illness.

Social workers are people-oriented workers who use a wide variety of techniques to help individuals and families cope with crises or to live fuller lives. They determine which helping methods to use by evaluating the nature of the problem, the amount of time available to work with the problem, and the available resources. Social workers also refer clients to other professionals or community resources. They use their training in human behavior, personality theory, and social group relations.

Some social workers are employed in such settings as family service or child welfare agencies. Social workers in these settings carry out the major responsibility of the setting. They may work with individuals, families, or groups. Social work services may involve direct counseling, supportive services, or referrals to other agencies or services.

Social workers also work in non–social-work settings. Schools hire social workers to help students whose family problems or personal problems interfere with education. Industry and business use social workers to help employees work out problems that interfere with work performance. Child guidance clinics, hospitals, and psychiatric institutions use social workers to provide social backgrounds that will help with patient diagnosis and with discharge planning.

The community health field (medicine and mental health) uses social workers in direct treatment, counseling, and taking social histories. In court systems and penal institutions, social workers participate in the rehabilitation process. In settlement houses, community centers, and youth organization agencies, social workers may become group leaders, administrators, or program specialists.

Social workers may help residents maintain maximum independence in residential institutions designed for people who cannot live by themselves, such as the aged, the severely handicapped, and those needing some type of intense training or treatment. The army hires social workers for rehabilitation for the disabled and for other social welfare programs.

In addition, social workers may work with a variety of public welfare concerns in social services, councils, social agencies, civil rights, and antipoverty roles. From these core programs, social workers go on to become involved in policy planning, administration, supervision, consultation, research, private practice, and various voluntary agencies.

Like many other fields, social work has some paraprofessional positions such as aides or technicians that require passing a test or completing a two-year community college human service program, but the basic entry-level requirement for social work is the four-year degree in social work—a B.S.W. from an accredited school. Even within this four-year educational period, you may choose to concentrate in a variety of areas including gerontology, criminal justice, psychology, growth and development, group work, or special issues.

With the master's degree, you prepare yourself for specialized study. At this stage you decide whether you are interested in medical social work, psychiatric social work, community organization, group work, or other areas of focused study. You become eligible for federal jobs and other specialized positions, or for promotion to supervisor. You also may choose to open a private practice as a clinical social worker. A Ph.D. degree opens more doors into teaching, research, and intense social work counseling and treatment.

A social worker's role is directly affected by what society sees as social issues and concerns. Jobs in the future will be affected by social trends. It is important to be looking not only at what is going on today, but in which direction our country seems to be heading.

Social work services have exploded in recent years. Social workers are involved in almost any setting with almost any problem or issue. You decide what kinds of people you want to work with, problems you want to deal with, or setting you want to work in. Your duties will depend on which setting you choose and what qualifications you possess. In all settings, however, you are involved with needs that society sees as problems or concerns. Regardless of your interests or concerns, social work offers you a variety of choices.

1

Historical Trends in Social Work

A social worker's role reflects changes in the economy, political climate, funding, and any legislative directives or social concerns. It is important to look at the historical developments to fully comprehend the influences of these changes. Understanding these influences will help you see how these changes can affect you as a social worker.

Religious Background

Caring for people developed into the role of the social worker. Religion played an important part in this notion of people caring for other people. This desire to help was practiced by major religions, such as Christianity and Judaism. During the Middle Ages, from about A.D. 400 to A.D. 1500, various religious groups devoted themselves to the tasks of healing or caring for the sick and feeding the poor. Unfortunately, after a while, this personal one-on-one caring just wasn't enough.

Industrial Revolution

From about the 1700s, new inventions and an increase in factory jobs began to draw people from the rural areas to the cities. As people moved into the cities, they also moved away from families and friends. Problems of overcrowding, unemployment, and poverty grew. More and more people became dependent on others for help in new settings where they received little or no family support.

At first, public relief, or welfare, was made as unattractive as possible. Almshouses or poorhouses, as they were called, were set up to collect or house the old, young, sick, mentally ill, blind, alcoholic, or anyone who was in need. Those who managed to avoid the poorhouse received help in their own homes, or outdoor relief. Any help received was considered the responsibility of the local parish, township, town, city, or county. Little state or colony supervision or control was permitted.

Charity Organization Society

During the 1800s, many private agencies were established to help people. One such agency, the Charity Organization Society, began in England. Knowledge of this program was brought to the United States, and one Reverend Gurteen founded a similar organization in Buffalo, New York, in 1877. This agency's program included the administration of charitable programs and the use of volunteers.

This organization began one of the first formal training programs for social work. In-service training was given to nurses, settlement workers, and the friendly visitors. The friendly visitors were usually young middle- to upper-class women. They were expected to become friends and advisors to poor families. They worked in schools, hospitals, and other charitable societies set up to help lower-class people. These fields of practices helped lay the basis for the organization of the profession of social work.

Similar training was done by other organizations by the early twentieth century. Training programs were also offered in colleges and universities. The New York School of Philanthropy (now called Columbia University School of Social Work) was the first school to train people for jobs with social agencies. This school was founded by the Charity Organization Society in 1898 in New York City. This type of training was continued into the 1940s.

The basic complaint about the earlier efforts of the voluntary agencies was that they tried to divide the needy into classes of worthy or unworthy. Problems also arose from trying to help people improve their lives without first helping them meet their basic needs.

Medical Social Work

The social welfare emphasis shifted in the 1800s from reform to exploring how the environment affects behavior. During this period, hospital social work was developed. In the early 1900s Dr. Richard Cabot monitored psychological and social factors. He wondered how these factors affected patients' reactions to their health problems and their willingness to use medical help. He thought that these factors should be treated as well as observed.

Social workers collected the results of social, psychological, and environmental information. When doctors were presented with this information, they found that they had a much better understanding of their patients. The specializations of medical and psychiatric social work developed from this practice.

Social Casework

Basic knowledge of social casework was also being developed in the 1920s. Of particular need were principles and concepts of helping that could be applied in all the different institutional areas or fields of practices. Mary Richmond was the first person to formulate social work practice in a systematic fashion. In her books *Social Diagnosis* and *What Is Social Casework?*, she described how one goes about helping people deal with social problems.

The theories of human behavior were integrated into social work. For example, Freudian and other psychological theories influenced our understanding and interpretation of how we react to things that happen around us.

Settlements

The work of social settlements also influenced the development of the profession of social work. Jane Addams and Florence Kelley were settlement leaders who lived with and experienced things with their clients. They didn't like the detachment of other professionals. They wanted to help change things through social reform (action) and social legislation (laws).

The settlement movement later helped develop social group work. Staffs, including college students volunteering their services, were expected to live in the areas that they served. The recipients were usually working-class people. Some settlement workers got involved in issues and actively supported organized labor movements. Services that they provided were usually educational and recreational in nature.

In their efforts to improve social conditions through social action and legislation, settlement workers tried to help struggling groups improve themselves and become part of mainstream society. The information exchanged with colleges helped in developing the social sciences.

An approach rather than a set of services described settlements. If someone came to the community from the outside, then that person and the settlement worked together to decide what was wrong and what was needed to help the situation. If the initiative came from within the community, then the program that was developed reflected the neighborhood's concerns about priorities and was more flexible.

Depending on the approach, the settlements pursued a number of different activities. They began many services such as clinics, convalescent homes, milk stations, and nursing services. They established camps and playgrounds. Settlement workers studied housing conditions, working hours, sanitation, sweatshops, and child labor. They used these studies to stimulate protective legislation. They also brought in such cultural activities as music, art, theater, and plays.

The settlement houses have changed over the years as needs have changed. Many things, such as playgrounds, adult classes, kindergartens, and health clinics, were taken over by public authorities. Other things, such as child labor, disappeared, and still others improved because of changes in legislation, such as the development of tenement standards. The areas of concern today are being refocused because of the changing trends. With the increasing number of elderly, for example, settlement houses are promoting such programs as "Meals on Wheels" and adult day care. Another concern is to help prepare youth for responsible parenthood. This is because the average age of sexual maturity has become much younger today than it has been in the past.

The settlements today are overseen by a national organization called the United Neighborhood Centers of America (UNCA).

Educational Influences

The history of charity organizations differed from the settlements in regard to higher education. Charities kept accurate statistics and written reports. They sponsored institutional and educational programs for the working. Affiliation with colleges developed when schools provided academic content and agencies provided practical experience. This practical experience is what was later called fieldwork.

In 1919 the Association of Training Schools for Professional Social Work was developed to deal with education for social work in an organized fashion. By 1952 this organization had developed into what is known today as the Council on Social Work Education (CSWE). This council is now the accrediting body for schools of social work.

By 1920 there were five fields of practice in social work. They were family, child welfare, medical, psychiatric, and school social work. Group work, leisure time services, community organization, corrections, and public assistance were added later.

Social Security Act

Income support and social services during the 1930s and 1940s were things the upper class provided for the so-called worthy poor.

In 1935 during the Great Depression, the United States government formed the Social Security Program. Under this program government became the major source of public aid. Changes in federal support for public assistance were set up to help the needy on the basis of right or entitlement rather than on being worthy or unworthy.

The entitlement concept stated that all people have the right to resources necessary for a decent life. It concluded that society must make these resources available to those who need them. This concept changed in definition and degree over the years as social and political concerns took on different meanings. Social work organizations supported entitlement programs that would help mothers and dependent children, the physically disabled, and the elderly.

The Social Security Act of 1935 marked the entry of the federal government into social welfare. Government then became the main support for the social welfare and social service programs. The voluntary agencies that hired most of the professional social workers or those with master's degrees in social work (M.S.W.) shifted their concerns to services other than financial aid. These included such services as family counseling and leisure time activities.

Social Work and Social Welfare

Many people see the influence of social welfare as a splitting of the field; that is, social welfare social work and professional social work began to represent different things and offer different services. To fully understand the field, concerns, and directions of the different agencies, you need to know what is meant by these two different concepts.

Social Work

Social work is the practice of helping people use their social environment to meet their needs. Social environment consists of any family, friends, groups, organizations, agencies, or government around a person. Social work, as such, wasn't really seen as a profession nor was the term used much until the early 1900s.

By the 1940s, social casework, social group work, and community organization became the three largest practice concentrations. Casework is direct contact between individuals and their families in need. Group work is working with several people at one time in a group setting. Community organization focuses on neighborhoods and larger groups of people.

Since the 1900s, these three areas have often been combined in social work practices. In fact, in 1955 seven associations, including the American Association of Social Workers (mostly caseworkers), the American Association of Group Workers, and the Association for the Study of Community Organization, joined to form what has become the largest social work association today, the National Association of Social Workers (NASW). A professional social worker had a master's degree in social work (M.S.W.) and the majority worked as social caseworkers.

It was also during this period that social workers became more concerned with the professionalism of their fields. Because of this, clinically oriented fields, such as the medical and psychiatric fields, attracted more of the educated social workers. The psychiatric social worker held the most status and prestige in the field. Because psychotherapy was considered mostly for the rich, many professional social workers weren't serving the needs of the most needy.

Social Welfare

The concept of social welfare goes back to the first organized efforts of the public to help its poor. It coincides with the Industrial Revolution and labor legislation from the eighteenth century. Social workers are professionals and the majority of them do work in the social welfare system. However, social welfare is an institutional arrangement that also uses many other professionals such as nurses, doctors, and psychologists.

The concerns of social workers have expanded into the entire social environment. Social workers have to know a great deal about the social systems they work in, including the social welfare system. They have to have skills in getting individuals and organizations to work together for the best interest of the client or families for whom they are working. Social welfare is only one of these systems that a social worker works in, but it is probably the one most people think about when they think of social work.

Although some people see social welfare as splitting the field of social work, social welfare is only one system that social workers work in. The splitting comes only because so many people equate social welfare work with social work. Social work principles have become foggy, and workers in welfare systems practice and carry out social welfare policies.

Civil Rights

The civil rights movement began with the 1954 decision of the United States Supreme Court declaring school segregation unconstitutional. This movement brought changes to the field of social work. Social workers supported the Black struggle for equal rights. During the 1960s this increased awareness of race and ethnicity brought a push for social equality for all groups. This concern spread to include many different social groups, such as women, the aged, children, prisoners, released offenders, mental patients, and students.

School Social Work

During the 1940s the role of social workers in school focused on diagnosing and treating difficult children. The visiting teacher program emphasized the need to acquaint teachers with the child's family and community life. Social workers in settlement houses were instrumental in calling for more social workers in schools. They were essential in identifying and responding to the needs of children in the educational process.

The mood also changed during the 1940s and the 1950s. The relationship between social work and education became supportive. School districts added services to help students and families cope with problems of the war and postwar years. This clinical orientation focused on the personal needs of the child and family rather than on the school and neighborhood.

The Mental Health Service Act of 1955 encouraged human service agencies in local communities to coordinate efforts to develop community mental health centers. Schools were also encouraged to develop links with community agencies. School social workers played a big part in connecting these links.

Radical changes took place in the 1960s. Technological change, the postwar population explosion, and the Vietnam War all challenged the human service practices. Schools needed to improve conditions to help prevent more violence from taking place in them. Social workers in schools helped change school policies to develop support systems in communities. Innovative methods of group work in schools were also practiced. The federal Elementary and Secondary Education Act (ESEA) of 1965 responded to what was seen as a natural crisis in education and the need to equalize education opportunities. Before this period, only local and state governments funded education. Title I of the ESEA provided financial assistance to state and local education agencies to enhance education in low-income areas. School social work expanded during this time.

Project Head Start in the mid-1960s offered educational and social programs to poor preschool children and their families. This program encouraged participation of parents. Social workers in schools helped increase parental involvement.

The Buckly Amendment to the Family Education Rights and Privacy Act of 1974 altered record keeping and highlighted confidentiality. As parents gained the right to know, social workers were asked to help interpret and discuss students' test results and recommendations with their parents.

In 1977 the National Association of Social Workers described three models of school social work:

1. The *traditional-clinical model* focuses on students with social/emotional problems. Students are considered clients.
2. The *school-change model* focuses on problems in the school's functioning and works to change school conditions, policies, and practices. Everyone in school is considered a client.
3. The *community-school relationship model* addresses experiences of inner-city schools and helps to develop under-

standing and support of school and community for one another. The whole school and community are considered clients.

Professional development and continuing education became important for the future in school social work practice. The first National Conference on School Social Work was held in 1978. It developed standards for specialization. Those who attended the conference demanded recognition and support from the whole profession of social work. They found the need to make political moves on their own behalf.

Paraprofessionals

President Johnson's "War on Poverty" in the 1960s brought about a couple of other changes in the roles of social workers. A number of jobs related to social work were created for persons regardless of education. With the economy strong, the federal government stimulated the development of social services. The supply of social workers was short. People who had no training in social work were hired to perform social work duties.

These paraprofessionals were usually quite effective working in their own neighborhoods with problems and people they were familiar with. Also during this time, community or junior colleges started two-year programs to provide technical training for para-professional social workers. Today people completing a two-year program may be eligible for an associate of arts degree (A.A.). With the aging population there are many more social work–related jobs in community organizations needing aides and technicians.

Clinical Social Work

During the 1960s the term *clinical social work* came into being. Social workers had been working in health care settings for more than eighty years. But during the social unrest of the 1960s, many social work clinicians believed that the schools of social work were focusing on the need for social change at the expense of preparation for clinical practice.

In 1972 the Social Security Act was amended to establish PSROs (Professional Standards Review Organizations) to review physicians' care of Medicaid and Medicare patients. The idea of this act was to limit unnecessary services and to encourage peer review, quality assurance, and accountability.

Social work was one of the nonmedical health care professions that anticipated PSRO involvement. Members of the profession worked to state their own accountability, quality assurance, and peer review. This preparation led to more of the following:

- effective case findings and discharge planning
- new skills and knowledge building
- accountability
- evaluation of services
- clarity of social work roles and tasks

By the mid-1970s this core of knowledge, values, and skills was accepted as a common base required for all practices.

Social workers responded to the commitment of high standards for clinical training and practice. The National Federation of Societies for Clinical Social Work was established. Clinical social workers' high professional standards for training and patient care contributed to their increasing acceptance in providing both physical and mental health services.

Schools of Social Work

During the 1970s, just as social work moved in many directions, the schools of social work also varied their training programs. Some schools still studied the three specialty areas of the 1940s, which were casework, group work, and community organization. Others trained generalists to use all methods to solve problems. Some focused on special problems, such as the aged, the poor, mental health, and minorities. Still other schools divided social work into the two distinct fields of direct and indirect services.

Until recently social work concentrated on the direct services, such as clinical therapy or social casework. Now indirect services are provided by practitioners, researchers, and scholars who develop, maintain, and reform the institution. In the late 1960s many schools of social work began a new type of training for social workers in community organization, social planning, social policy analysis, and administration.

Direct Services

As already mentioned, social workers work directly with people in one of three ways: casework, group work, and community organization. Many social workers have to deal with all three functions. In direct services you may work with individuals and their problems on a one-to-one basis, with families or small groups, or with larger groups. You may also be involved in community work.

Indirect Services

Social workers who perform services on behalf of people rather than directly with them provide indirect services. Previously, social workers were not trained in such areas as management and programs evaluation. Today, however, their jobs can entail working in administration, policy making, or teaching. Such social workers might direct or design programs. Also, with other professional staff they might develop policy and procedures to improve the delivery of services. They might work with community agencies and teach staff or students. Indirect services may mean doing research, program evaluation, policy analysis, and statistical analysis. It may also mean coordinating social services with other services, developing budgets, conducting audits, or performing some management duties.

Council on Social Work Education

In 1952 a private accreditation agency called the Council on Social Work Education was established. All graduate schools must be accredited and periodically reviewed by this council. In 1961 the National Association of Social Workers (NASW) established a level of training needed in social work. This certification was called the Academy of Certified Social Workers (ACSW). It was determined that undergraduate education should have courses to help develop students' knowledge of:

- human growth and behavior
- society and social interaction
- philosophy of social welfare

- social welfare as an institution
- social work as a profession
- methods of problem solving
- communication

In 1970 the NASW recognized social workers with accredited baccalaureate degrees (B.S.W.) as regular members of the association if they completed such a program for a social work major as approved by the Council on Social Work Education. By 1973 the NASW had set up standards of classification for paraprofessional and professional levels of social service workers.

They based the professional social work practice on the B.S.W. Three further levels of practice were the M.S.W. (the master's degree in social work), the A.C.S.W. (the certified social worker), and the social work fellow (the advanced degree). Two paraprofessional levels were identified: social service aide, which required no formal education beyond high school; and the social service technician, which required either an associate of arts degree in a human service program or a major in human services in a baccalaureate program.

In 1983 the NASW established the National Peer Review Advisory Committee. It trains social workers to evaluate the work of other social workers. This helps to promote accountability and meet quality control requirements of the government and other funding organizations. The Council on Social Work Education also issued a Curriculum Policy Statement for the baccalaureate as well as master's degree programs in social work education.

The ACBSW, or the Academy of Certified Baccalaureate Social Workers, was established in 1991.

Public Assistance

Until 1972 there were four major categories of needy people who received help from public assistance programs. These categorical programs were Old Age Assistance, Aid to the Blind, Aid to the Totally Disabled, and Aid to Families with Dependent Children. These programs, though funded by federal, state, and local monies, were run by the states.

In 1972 the federal government took over the major responsibilities for the aged, the blind, and disabled adults under a program called Supplementary Security Income (SSI). This program was meant to supplement the financial needs of adults whose basic needs weren't covered by Social Security. The Social Security system handled the SSI program.

Another income program, called General Assistance, was supported only by state and local funds. This program was meant to help people financially who didn't meet the requirements of the Social Security or public assistance program.

Social Services

Today social welfare services are viewed as services that should be offered to everyone, not just the poor. These middle-class entitlement programs have expanded considerably. Title XX (the 1974 amendment to the Social Security Act) set up a legislative framework for states to provide social services for everyone. Under this legislation, the states are required to offer some services, such as protection services and information and referral, to everyone. In fact, the amendment allows states to offer almost any service they might choose to people who are well into the middle-income range.

Social services are programs that help people deal with a variety of social problems. In Title XX, forty distinct categories of services are found, such as child welfare, day care, protective services, counseling, information and referral, family planning, and services to the aged.

Block Grants

Block grants were given to states in the early 1980s. With these grants states have more responsibility in determining and controlling services. But with these grants also come federal guidelines that have to be followed for the states to be eligible to receive these monies. For example, under Medical Assistance, waivers are given for preadmission screening for potential residents to nursing homes. Under this guideline, a preadmission assessment team of a public health nurse and a social worker evaluates each person who is being considered for nursing home care who is or will be eligible for medical assistance within 180 days. This assessment team determines whether nursing home care is needed or if home health services would meet the client's needs instead. The final choice is up to the client and his or her family.

Another federal regulation affecting care and payment is in respite care (outside care to relieve the regular caregiver of a sick or disabled person for a temporary period). Let's say a nursing home gets $60 a day for respite care. Under the federal guideline for respite care, a nurse would determine how much self-care a patient can manage. If a patient can handle a great deal of self-care, the nursing home would get reimbursed only a percentage of the total grant for patient care. The home may get only $35 to $40 instead of $60 for full care.

Because of these increasing federal regulations, it is possible that fewer services may be offered. A nursing home that could take in a full-time resident is less likely to leave a bed available for a questionable payment for respite care. Of course, if bed space is available this wouldn't be as much of a concern. Other regulations demand much lighter caseload ratios. A ratio of one social worker to twenty-five cases may be required, especially in areas that the federal government has determined are high priority. Recently some high-priority areas have included services for chemical dependency (CD), for mental retardation (MR), for mental illness (MI), and for home health care.

In addition to requiring certain social worker/client ratios, the federal regulations are demanding that a more qualified person work in these special areas (CD, MR, MI). This person may be required to have four hundred hours of supervised work with, say, the mentally retarded, to be qualified to work alone with them.

These federal requirements of smaller social worker/client ratios, more qualified personnel, preadmission screening, and paying according to the services actually needed sound like a dream for social workers and a relief for taxpayers. But smaller agencies and poorer counties don't always have qualified staff in all the specialized areas, nor can they afford enough staff to handle these ratios. And with federal monies come requirements. Although the states have the funds to do as they see best, the best is still being determined at the federal level.

Family Services Administration

In 1986 the Family Services Administration was created as a unit within the U.S. Department of Health and Human Services. It consolidated the six major federal low-income programs:

Aid to Families with Dependent Children (AFDC)
Work Incentive Program
Community Service Block Grants
Low-Income Home Energy Assistance
Refugee Assistance
Child Support Enforcement Program

Voluntary Social Services

Voluntary services are a network of social welfare services supported by voluntary or private resources. They are not supported by public funds. Voluntary agencies provide social services to communities as needs arise. They may provide services similar to those of public agencies or they may specialize in areas and concerns of special needs. Since they are private agencies, they may have religious affiliations, such as Catholic Charities and Lutheran Social Services.

Trends for Services

Many social workers use a combination of casework, group work, and community organization as well as administrative and other indirect services. In fact, in many settings, a person has to be able to use all areas of functioning.

Today a social worker usually concentrates in a service area or specialization, such as mental health, medical health, aging, corrections, school social work, or social welfare. There are many settings within each of these concentrations:

- A person in *mental health* might work in the psychiatric ward of a local hospital, in a state mental health hospital, in private practice, or in a mental health clinic.

- A person in *medical health* may work in the social service department in a local hospital, in a clinic, in a local community health center, or in a health system agency.
- A social worker in *corrections* may work in a probation office, in a social service agency, in a prison or correctional facility, or in a community program.
- A *school* social worker may be found in a nursery school, in an elementary school, in a high school, in a vocational technical school, or in a college.
- A *social welfare* worker may be found in a welfare or social service department, in a private social service agency, or in a community agency.
- Other *specialized services* may be found in industrial settings, in services for the aging, in social group work, or in community organization work.

2

SOCIAL WORK QUALIFICATIONS

SOCIAL WORK IN its pure form, in its substance, is a defined profession. But the roles of social workers are greatly defined by the field or setting in which these workers are involved.

Social work covers a wide variety of services and fields of practice. A person may specialize in many different kinds of social services. Usually the applicant's formal education determines the level of responsibility. It also determines the advancement opportunities.

As you explore the field of social work, it would help to understand what specific training and qualifications you will need for each level of the profession. Whether you choose an associate, bachelor's, master's, or doctorate degree, you will find social work to be a challenging, demanding, and very fulfilling profession.

Professional Levels/Degrees

Social work is usually categorized within two main groups: paraprofessional and professional. According to the National Association of Social Workers (NASW), a paraprofessional level may be classified as a social service aide or a social service technician. A social service aid is evaluated and hired on experience and such personal attributes as maturity, appropriate life experiences, motivation, and skills needed for the job. A social service technician usually has completed a two-year educational program in social service and has an associate of arts degree. A professional position requires a B.S.W. (baccalaureate of social work), an M.S.W. (master's of social work), or higher education and related experience.

Professional Levels of Practice

The NASW's description of the four levels of social work professional are:

- *Basic Professional Level* requires a bachelor's degree (B.S.W.) from a social work program accredited by the Council on Social Work Education (CSWE).
- *Specialized (Expert) Professional Level* requires a master's degree (M.S.W.) from a social work program accredited by CSWE.
- *Independent Professional Level* represents an accredited M.S.W. and at least two years of experience following the master's degree under appropriate professional supervision.
- *Advanced Professional Level* requires proficiency in specialized areas or the ability to conduct advanced research studies in social welfare; this is usually demonstrated through a

doctorate degree in social work or a closely related social science discipline.

Associate Degree

An associate of science degree may be similar to that offered at Pikes Peak Community College in Colorado Springs, Colorado. The degree is called "Social Services Technician." The name of the degree and the specific courses may vary from college to college and state to state. This particular two-year social services degree offers courses in social welfare and community agencies, intervention techniques, human behavior, and group counseling.

This degree is only one of many specializations, but it serves as an example of a two-year social services program. The following is a sample of the types of courses that may be taken at a two-year community college.

General education courses
Communication
   English
   Speech
Physical education/health
   Health
   First aid safety
Humanities
Math/science
   Biology
Social science
   Psychology
   Sociology

Psychology courses
Psychology of adjustment
Human behavior
Child psychology
Adolescent psychology
Adulthood and aging

Electives
Human sexuality
Survey of disabilities
Alcohol/drug/narcotics abuse
Social problems
Marriage and family
Death and dying

Personal development courses
Career courses
    Survey of human services
    Planning goals and objectives
    Helping skills
    Group process
    Internship
Introduction to computer-based system
CPR

B.S.W. Degree

A bachelor's degree is usually the minimum requirement for professional positions in the field. In fact, some states that formerly required a master's degree for public positions now only require a bachelor's degree. This declassification process has opened up some positions for four-year degree social workers. Other undergraduate majors in psychology, sociology, and related fields may satisfy the requirements of many social service agencies.

In 2002 there were 421 accredited B.S.W. programs according to statistics provided by the Council on Social Work Education. The B.S.W. degree prepares students for direct service positions, such as a caseworker or a group worker. Classroom instruction is offered in social work practice, social welfare policies, human behavior, social environment, and social research methods. All accredited programs require four hundred hours of supervised field experience.

A social work major is designed to prepare a student to become an entry-level professional social worker and/or to enter graduate school. Courses are taught by social workers in a variety of practice fields. The program should be accredited by the Council on Social Work Education.

The B.S.W. helps prepare a student to enter employment in many fields of practice including: mental health, county social services, medical social work, corrections, probation and parole, residential treatment, school social work, outreach and youth counseling, nursing home social work, social work with migrants, and family planning.

One such accredited B.S.W. social work program, from Bemidji State University in Minnesota, offers a suggested academic schedule:

Freshman year
General biology
General psychology
Introduction to sociology
Introduction to social welfare
Field experiences in social work
General education courses

Sophomore year
Interpersonal behavior
Human behavior in the social environment
Social welfare policy
Modern social programs
Ethnic and minority group relations
Abnormal psychology
Child psychology
Adolescent psychology
Social gerontology
General education courses and electives

Junior/senior years
Social work practice I, II, III
Internship orientation
Internship in social work
Social statistics
Methods of social research
Theory electives
At least one of the following:
    Bureaucracy and society
    Social psychology
    Social class and stratification
    Contemporary sociology theory

M.S.W. Degree

A master's in social work (M.S.W.) is generally required for positions in the mental health field, and it is almost always needed for supervisory, research, or administrative positions. The M.S.W.

degree is preferred for clinical positions and is essential for social workers in private practice.

In 2002 there were 139 accredited M.S.W. programs. A typical M.S.W. program will include two years of specialized study, including nine hundred hours of supervised field instruction or internship. This field placement helps students determine whether they are suited for social work practice. This experience may also help develop an expertise in a specialized area. Also, field experience is useful for making personal contacts, who may later help you to secure a job.

Neither previous training in social work nor a B.S.W. degree in social work is required for entry into an M.S.W. graduate program. Courses in psychology, sociology, economics, political science, history, social anthropology, and urban studies, as well as social work, are recommended. Some graduate schools offer an accelerated M.S.W. program for qualified applicants. Persons who have received a B.S.W. undergraduate degree from an accredited program of social work may be qualified for such an accelerated program.

Ph.D. Degree

A person with a Ph.D. degree would be considered for a position in teaching, research, or administration. Although a master's degree will allow you to go into private practice and clinical social work, a Ph.D. degree is desired for some clinical positions and for additional specialization in the field. It is also desirable for a person in the field of intensive social work counseling and treatment. In 2002 there were seventy-one doctorate programs in the United States. The Council on Social Work Education does not accredit doctorate programs.

Personal Abilities

What is a social worker? What does it take to be a social worker? How do you know if you have what it takes? Think about who you are, how you are growing, and for what goals you are reaching. You should have or be able to obtain the following qualities:

- emotional maturity
- objectivity
- sensitivity
- concern for people and their problems
- sincere respect for all human beings
- capacity to handle responsibility
- ability to work independently
- ability to interact with people

You should be interested in and able to acquire the skills and abilities to:

- help people work out problems
- help people adjust to difficult situations
- establish rapport to meet clients' needs
- communicate effectively
- maintain good working relationships with clients and coworkers
- listen effectively
- be able to see a situation from another person's point of view, regardless of your own feelings
- be dedicated to keep standards high

The NASW has prepared a list entitled "Knowledge, Skills, Abilities, and Values for Social Work Practice." This list gives a good indication of what a potential social worker should strive to obtain.

Registration Versus Licensure

In the profession you often hear the terms "registered social worker" and "licensed social worker." What is the difference? Registration is a title protection and regulates the use of the name "social worker." Licensure regulates both the title and the practice of social work. Licensure is considered a form of public protection as it regulates the scope of practice and the conduct of those who practice social work. All fifty states now have licensing or registration, and thirty-three have vendorship laws regarding social work practice and the use of professional titles.

Licensure

Requirements for and definition of social workers vary from state to state. For example, the Minnesota Board of Social Workers lists standards for licensure in four categories:

- Social worker—bachelor's degree in social work
- Graduate social worker—master's or doctorate degree in social work
- Independent social worker—master's or doctorate degree in social work and two years of supervised practice in social work
- Independent clinical social worker—master's or doctorate degree in a social work program of clinically oriented course work and two years of supervised practice in social work

Licensees must have degrees from an accredited program of social work education, pass an examination, meet requirements for supervision, conduct all professional activities in accordance with ethical standards, and complete forty-five hours of continuing education for each three-year period. Requirements for licensure may vary; contact your state's social work board for its requirements.

The American Association of State Social Work Boards is an organization of the boards in states and territories that regulate social work. It was formed in 1979 to share information among the states and territories. Contact them for your state's Social Work Board's address and phone number.

American Association of State Social Work Boards
400 South Ridge Parkway, Suite B
Culpeper, VA 22701
(540) 829-6880
aswb.org

State Licensing Versus Credentialing

State licensing requires minimum competency to protect the public and regulates the use of the social work title and practice. States may require licensing to practice social work. Social work credentials such as the ACBSW, ACSW (Academy of Certified Social Workers), Qualified Clinical Social Worker, the Diplomate in Clinical Social Work, or the School Social Work Specialist are not required, although they may give you a competitive edge.

In 1991 the NASW created the Academy of Certified Baccalaureate Social Workers (ACBSW) to give the B.S.W. national professional recognition. This was modeled after the ACSW. The ACBSW requirements include:

- a baccalaureate degree in social work accredited by the Council on Social Work Education (CSWE)
- a minimum of two years postgraduation supervised social work employment
- completed performance evaluation from a supervisor and a professional social work colleague
- submission of an official copy of school transcripts
- agreement to practice according to NASW code of ethics, practice, and standards and to submit to adjudication proceedings if charged with violations
- successful completion of the ACBSW examination and payment of fees

The NASW offers voluntary certification and awards membership in the Academy of Certified Social Workers (ACSW). The requirements for ACSW membership include:

- a master's or doctorate degree from a school of social work accredited by the CSWE
- two years of full-time or three thousand hours of equivalent part-time paid postmaster's or postdoctorate social work experience with supervision by a social worker in an agency or organized setting

NASW membership requirements include:

- completion of the supervisory evaluation form and two professional references from social work colleagues
- appropriate forms and fee payments
- successful completion of the ACSW examination

The NASW also registers clinical social workers both as Qualified Clinical Social Workers (QCSW) and Diplomate in Clinical Social Work (DCSW). Since 1976 the NASW identifies qualified clinical social workers who meet NASW standards for clinical practice. The NASW created the Diplomate in Clinical Social Work in 1986 to distinguish advanced clinical practice expertise. As of 2002 more than eighty thousand members of NASW have earned ACSW, DCSW, and QCSW credentials.

One of the newest credentials is the "School Social Work Specialist" credential, first awarded in 1992. It is available for those social workers who work in public schools, private schools, preschools, special education, and residential school settings.

Other new specialty certifications offered by the NASW in 2002 are "Certified-Clinical Alcohol, Tobacco and Other Drugs Social Worker" (C-CATODSW), "Certified-Advanced Social Work Case Manager" (C-ASWCM), and "Certified-Social Work Case Manager" (C-SWCM).

Private Practice/Clinical Social Work

In each field of practice you must meet specific qualifications. Private practice in clinical social work demands special qualifications plus other considerations. Two major professional directories provide objective guidelines in the field of clinical social work: the *National Registry of Health Care Providers in Clinical Social Work* and the *National Association of Social Workers (NASW) Register of Clinical Social Workers*.

Both of these registries require a master's degree, two years of full-time work in direct service, knowledge of legal requirements, and responsibility for self-appraisal.

In 1986 a board certification program was announced in the National Registry. This is for clinical social workers who have practiced clinical social work for at least five years and who have passed a test in clinical social work practice. Many states require the legal regulation of social work practice; some states require a special license for practitioners of clinical social work as well as for those in independent private practice. Generally certification for clinical social work requires a master's degree in social work plus at least two years of experience and successful completion of an examination.

Supervision

Individuals going into private practice need to be able to provide themselves with the tools for professional growth. Especially during the first few years, you need to find someone willing (on a fee basis) to consult with you and serve in a supervisory role. This supervisory or psychiatric consultation is reassuring to practitioners in the early stages of practice. Supervisors may offer experience and objective perspectives. They also offer insights to complex problems.

You will need to keep in touch with others in the field in similar roles for support and exchange of ideas. It is equally important to keep up with current literature, attend workshops, and get advanced training. All these things are important as you learn about and cope with your own difficulties in dealing with all aspects of private practice. It is all part of accepting responsibility for the client and the field of practice.

Business Aspects

Like any business venture, setting up private practice involves certain housekeeping details that are also important. These include:

- office space
- privacy (yours and the clients')
- source of clientele
- record keeping
- fees
- learning about resources that are available
- becoming familiar with malpractice and avoiding it

A good way to become familiar with issues, concerns, and information is to join an association and related organizations in your field of practice or interest. For clinical social work you may wish to contact:

Clinical Social Work Federation
P.O. Box 3740
Arlington, VA 22203
(703) 522-3866
cswf.org

This organization should be able to tell you whether there is a local association for clinical social work in your state.

Other Resources

Contact other associations or organizations for information in your specific field (see Appendixes A and B). Also subscribe to or read related professional journals (see Appendix C). If possible, find individuals who are working in the role that you are interested in and ask them if you may interview them about their profession.

Many professionals are eager and willing to talk about what they do, if they can arrange the time.

Another way to learn about the specifics of your field of practice would be to study the pamphlets on the *Ethics and Standards of Practices* published by the NASW.

Specifically for private practice, ask for:

Standards for Practice of Clinical Social Work
Standards for Continuing Professional Education

Other professional or practice standards offered by the NASW are:

Code of Ethics
Professional Credentials
Standards for Social Work in Health Care Settings
Standards for Social Work Personnel Practices
Standards for Social Work in Long-Term Care Facilities
Standards for Social Work Practice in Child Protection
Standards for School Social Work Services
Bylaws of the National Association of Social Workers

For information on how to obtain copies of these and other professional materials contact:

National Association of Social Workers
750 First Street NE, Suite 700
Washington, D.C. 20002-4241
(800) 638-8799
socialworkers.org

For information on Canadian social work, see Chapter 8, "Social Work Opportunities in Canada," and Appendix B, "Canadian Associations." Additional information can be obtained from:

Canadian Association of Social Workers
383 Parkdale Avenue, Suite 402
Ottawa, ON K1Y 4R4
Canada
(613) 729-6668
casw-acts.ca

Areas that are opening up for private practitioners may be found with support groups for families of patients who are suffering from a specific or chronic illness, such as Alzheimer's disease, AIDS, or cancer. There are also support groups for families burdened with care of the elderly, handicapped, and retarded family members and for people in need of short-term treatment for stress or change.

State Qualifications

Each state has qualification guidelines for employment in various settings. Contact any local agency or professional organization in your area and ask for the address of the licensing department for your field of interest for your state. Jobs may be available by meeting qualifications of various testing and placement systems such as:

Civil Service listing for federal, state, or county positions
Merit System for some county listings
State Personnel, Licensing, and Placement Department
State Board of Social Workers

You may find out about these systems in your state by contacting your state's job service (for federal, state, and local positions), federal offices (for federal positions), county offices (for county positions), State Department of Education (for positions in the education system, such as school social workers), or your public library (for addresses of appropriate contacts).

3

AREAS OF SOCIAL WORK

SOCIAL WORK IS a profession for those who have a strong need to help others improve their lives. Social workers are found in any location where people work with people. Where you work will affect your duties, the way things are handled, your working conditions, the method of social work practice used, and the types of clients you will be working with.

Many settings hire social workers who have doctorate, master's, and bachelor's degrees, as well as paraprofessional workers. Your qualifications determine your responsibilities and duties. You may work in almost any setting with a wide range of qualifications. A hospital setting might use a social worker with an associate of arts degree in its recreation program, a worker with a bachelor's degree (B.S.W.) in discharge planning and follow-up, and a medical or psychiatric social worker in treatment.

On the other hand, social workers with identical qualifications may work in quite different settings. A clinical social worker may be employed in an industrial employee-assistance program, in a mental health center, or in private practice. Therefore, it is important to know in what settings social workers are employed and what duties are expected. Being familiar with different places that hire social workers may help you decide where your own talents and interests will best be used.

Being familiar with settings and knowing what services they provide might also help determine what kind of schooling, field practice, or work experience you should be considering. Not all social workers have the capability or the desire to work in all fields of social work. A person may thrive in a job working with foster care and adoption but find it difficult dealing with, for example, teenagers or the elderly. The more experiences you have with people, the better you will be able to evaluate your own strong points and interests.

This chapter describes some of the main areas of interest. Some settings and programs within these areas of interest are explored. Schools of thought differ in how to classify the social work field. As we explore this field, we will look at these areas of social work:

- family and child welfare and social services
- services for the aging
- mental health
- medical health
- corrections
- school social work
- community organizations and group work
- private practice

Requirements and duties differ among states and among agencies. But a general description of the basic philosophies, concerns, and services offered by various settings will give you a good understanding of areas that social workers are involved in.

Family and Child Welfare Services

The area of social services (public and voluntary services) is the largest employer of social workers. Availability of funds through taxes (public) and through private donations (voluntary) helps decide how many services will be provided and who will be served. Public services depend on which services the government mandates as must-provide services and the amount of funding the government grants for these services. Also, social work specializations and the services they provide vary with changes in social concerns.

Voluntary family services are also included in this group. Services provided through voluntary agencies are similar to public services, but funding sources and other emphases may differ. Three main areas of services provided in the social service/social welfare services are services for family, child welfare, and public assistance.

Voluntary Social Services

Voluntary family service agencies, be they private for-profit or private not-for-profit, offer many similar services. Unlike public social service agencies, voluntary agencies such as Catholic Charities, Jewish Services, Lutheran Social Services, and the Salvation Army may have a religious background and purpose. They may also offer services free, for a fee, or on a sliding-scale fee (fees depending upon ability to pay). They may be funded by a certain church body or parent organization, by United Way funds, or by private donations. Other private voluntary agencies may be funded totally through fees and insurance coverage.

Service provided by some voluntary agencies may specialize in such social issues and needs as the following:

- marriage preparation
- individual and family counseling
- marriage counseling
- financial counseling
- pregnancy counseling
- adoption services
- emergency assistance
- food shelf
- refugee assistance
- clothing and furniture assistance
- family life education
- social concerns and ministry
- farm peer counselors
- services for the handicapped
- services for the aging
- residential treatment homes
- family services

Public Social Services/Social Welfare Services

Unlike voluntary services, public social services receive most of their monies through taxes. Services are provided to some clients, who are not eligible for free services, on a sliding-scale fee basis. Some services like protection and information and referral (I&R) are offered to everyone. A public social service department or a public welfare agency may offer many services and monies as mandated by federal, state, or local governments. Three main areas are income maintenance programs, social service programs, and block grants and referral services.

Income maintenance programs
supplemental assistance programs
Aid to Families with Dependent Children (AFDC)
general assistance (GA)
general assistance, medical
medical assistance (MA)
food stamp program
energy assistance

Social service programs
adoption service
counseling service for families and individuals
day care licensing
employability services
foster care services for children and adults
homemaking services
information and referral services
protection services—children and adults
residential treatment referrals
transportation services
court-order custody studies and mediations

Block grants and referral services
assessment service MI, CD, or MR (mentally ill,
    chemically dependent, or mentally deficient/retarded)

occupational training centers
community action rural transportation
halfway houses

Family and Child Services

Services are provided to families during emergencies or when something happens to upset the normal functioning of the family. This might be caused by an illness in the family, the sudden absence of one or both parents, or the unemployment of the main wage earner. Social workers help individuals or families whose lives are affected by poverty, alcoholism, drug abuse, behavioral problems, or illnesses. Funding determines the kinds of services that social and welfare institutions may offer to people. There are guidelines that determine who is eligible for services.

Child Welfare and Protection Service

Child welfare services are said to be a profession in the service of an ideal. This practice is based on the belief that problems can best be worked out by treating the family as a unit. Child welfare is a specialization in the field of social welfare. Although the whole family is the major concern, child welfare concentrates on children who are dependent, neglected, or abused.

Child welfare services differ from services for children. Child welfare services are provided under the public welfare system. Social work with children may be set up in schools, community mental health centers, and family service agencies. Child welfare services deal directly with the actual protection and care of the child rather than services for the child.

Public Assistance

The income maintenance or public assistance units of the welfare system are concerned with evaluating whether people are eligible for public monies. They may evaluate eligibility for programs such as money payments, food stamps, medical care, or other general assistance. They may also identify needs and make referrals to social services and other agencies or community resources.

In a voluntary system, the assistance program might evaluate eligibility for other services, such as reduced fees for counseling, food shelves, donated clothing, free or reduced meals, or emergency funding. Depending upon the setting and complexity of the position, income maintenance workers may be social service aides or technicians rather than social workers.

Aging and Elderly Services

Although aging could be listed under services to families, aging has become a separate field of study on its own. There are many settings just for the elderly. Modern technology and improved medicine and living conditions all add to the increasing population of the elderly. Gerontology, the study of aging, is a growing field, and studies have been made of the changes in the structure and functions of bodies due to the aging process. Other age-related studies have been done on the following topics:

- social status
- roles
- behavior

- living arrangements
- political participation
- retirement
- income
- cultural activities
- minority concerns
- adjustments to living

Other areas of concern for the aging population are how its members are affected by the following social institutions: the economy, welfare, health and medical care systems, government organizations and functions, education, and the demographic structure of society.

Social workers who specialize in the field of aging plan and evaluate services for the elderly. They may also help older people, as well as their families, deal with difficulties brought on by their declining health and changing circumstances. In a nursing home, for example, a social worker may help patients and their families adjust to the need for long-term institutional care. The social worker would also be available to help with any planning and emotional difficulties related to this change.

Social workers are found in every aspect of social services for the aging. These services may be found in group medical practices, community mental health centers, travel agencies, personnel offices of large agencies, educational facilities, employment agencies, and other investment and media agencies. Some private practitioners are specializing in services for the elderly, too.

Social workers are also employed in the following places:

- adult day care centers
- community planning agencies

- hospices
- nursing homes
- retirement centers
- Veterans Administration hospitals
- legislative bodies
- nutrition sites
- older-worker employment programs
- community care agencies
- senior citizens centers
- national aging networks

Social work with the elderly helps alleviate negative aspects of aging. The goal of such social work is to help the older person achieve a better quality of life.

Mental Health Facilities

The mental health field is the one that attracts the most social workers. People in this field include clinical social workers, psychiatric social workers, and other mental health workers. People in this field usually work to develop community residential facilities and supportive services for the mentally disabled. They may provide services in the following areas: outreach, crisis intervention, social rehabilitation, and training in skills in everyday living.

The main institutions that hire social workers in the mental health specialization are Veterans Administration hospitals, state mental health facilities, private psychiatric hospitals, and psychiatric units of general hospitals. Mental health clinics and drop-in centers also present career opportunities.

Since the mid-1980s the accelerating cost of hospital care and increased competition has shortened hospital (psychiatric) care service. Inpatient psychiatric social workers have been affected, and many have been laid off. Other social workers have had to make major changes in what they do on the job and have had responsibility in implementing the changes.

The definitions of both long-term and short-term work have changed. Rather than working toward "change," the goal of hospitalization was to stabilize or return the patient to the prehospital condition. Short-term work now generally involves education, rehabilitation, and direct problem-solving techniques. Previously these were used for involved observation, interpretation, and behavior modification. Social workers have coped with changes in psychiatric inpatient care by learning new techniques, redefining their jobs, and limiting expectations and goals.

Mental Health Centers

Mental health centers are located in many communities and employ social workers along with psychiatrists and psychologists. The centers provide services to people on the basis of ability to pay. They may receive monies through block grants from the counties or the states. They work cooperatively with other community services, such as social services, schools, hospitals, and rehabilitation and employment agencies. The services that they offer include the following:

- information, education, and cooperation
- consultations
- outpatient diagnostic services
- outpatient treatment and rehabilitation
- emergency and residential services
- cooperation with hospital mental health units

- marriage counseling
- individual counseling

Veterans Administration Hospitals

Veterans Administration hospitals (VA hospitals) are regional hospitals for veterans. Each hospital has its own specialization of services. One hospital may specialize in psychiatric services, another in services for the elderly, and another in heart care and surgery. Social work is a clinical service that works within this hospital community.

The primary mission of social service within this community is to reduce or remove psychosocial barriers for a successful hospital treatment and recovery. The social service staff may work in all areas of this medical center as team members with other professionals such as nurses, psychologists, psychiatrists, and doctors. They work with veterans and their families, helping with inpatient and outpatient treatment.

Services may involve one-on-one or group counseling. Services are designed to reduce stress due to medical problems. Some of these services include:

- application for financial benefits
- links to other community services
- family counseling
- adjustment to a changed lifestyle
- employment counseling

Services offered would reflect the specialization of the particular hospital. VA hospitals are communities in themselves and offer a wide range of services:

- *Chaplain services* provide a program of spiritual care and counseling for patients; opportunities are provided for worship, counseling, education, and crisis care.
- *Dental services* provide a full range of dental treatment.
- *Dietetic service* meets the nutritional needs of the patients.
- *The education office* is responsible for the overall organization and coordination of the facility's education programs, patient education, library service, and media services.
- *Patient advocacy* is available to all patients to provide information, assist with problems, and act in the patients' best interests when required.
- *Medical service* provides a wide range of medical treatment programs on both an inpatient and outpatient basis.
- *Nursing services* provide direct personal care of patients.
- *Psychiatry services* provide treatment for inpatients and outpatients suffering from neurotic and psychotic disorders of both an acute and a chronic nature.
- *The chemical dependency center* provides care both for veterans involved in problems with chemical dependency and for their families.
- *The day treatment center* is a partial hospitalization program designed to provide services for veterans having difficulties with emotional problems, community adjustment, interpersonal relations, and vocational or educational problems. This center serves as a buffer between the hospital and the community. It allows patients to move back into community life at their own pace.
- *Psychology service* is provided to veterans in all parts of the medical center.
- *Recreation services* are provided as therapeutic and leisure education and as other programs that serve as

part of a continuum of care for both inpatient and outpatient status.

- *Rehabilitation medicine services* use physical, psychosocial, and vocational activities for the prevention and diagnosis of disease and treatment of veterans with physical or mental handicaps. These activities may include such disciplines as corrective therapy, occupational therapy, physical therapy, speech pathology/audiology, and vocational rehabilitation therapy.

- *Volunteer services* supplement the activities of the regular staff by relieving the professional personnel of duties not requiring professional training.

State Mental Health Hospitals

State hospitals are multiservice facilities for the residential care of mentally handicapped, chemically dependent, or mentally ill persons. Some facilities may specialize in one or more of these services. The hospitals provide programs for the educable mentally handicapped or emotionally disturbed. These hospitals, or regional human service centers as some are called, have publicly funded services.

People receive treatment on an around-the-clock basis, similar to services provided by VA hospitals and private psychiatric hospitals. Drop-in centers also provide mental health services, but on a crisis or need basis. Like other hospitals, these hospitals provide some community-like services. They provide routine medical and dental services, but patients would have to go to larger hospitals for major surgery or other more highly sophisticated treatment. These hospitals are narrower in their scope and provide mainly mental health services. They work with community resources in setting up service plans for the patients.

Other Residential Treatment Centers

Institutional or substitutional care of an individual occurs when a person must be cared for out of the home for twenty-four hours a day because of some special need. This residential treatment includes not only day-to-day care and supervision, but provides treatment for the emotionally disturbed or mentally deficient as well.

A residential treatment center may be a hospital, such as a state or private hospital, or it may be a local center or home in the community, such as a group home or foster home. Group homes are licensed to care for groups of people with emotional or mental handicaps. Individual homes with specially qualified adults, such as foster homes, may also be used to care for children or adults with special needs. Other residential care facilities may be found in schools for the deaf, for the blind, and for other physically handicapped children.

A residential staff's responsibilities and duties will depend on the specialty and treatment offered by the center or home. Some services provided by social workers will be teaching direct living skills, supervision and support of other staff, consultation, or direct therapy. They will work closely with other staff such as caregivers, medical workers, and other therapists.

Social workers may also be involved with licensing of such homes as foster homes, group homes, and other community located centers. Their responsibilities may include arranging for financial payment, giving information to families about the services, providing supportive services, and referring eligible clients.

Medical Settings

Social workers may also work in hospitals, hospices, health maintenance organizations, nursing homes, rehabilitation centers, and offices of physicians. Social workers in the medical setting may be caseworkers, medical social workers, or clinical social workers. Other health-related positions might be found in home health, clinics, and other health care areas.

Nursing Homes

Nursing homes are long-term treatment institutions that care for people who are unable to provide for their own personal needs. These homes provide health care, rooms, eating facilities, and prepared nutritional foods. Some homes provide recreational, social, and occupational activities; therapy; entertainment; and a wide selection of services, many of which are provided by volunteers from the community.

Some homes are licensed to care for people needing more intensive care. Others offer more or less board-and-room type of care with available nursing staff. Smaller homes have consulting social workers, usually through a larger nursing home or a local hospital. They may also use a social service agency. Larger homes have their own social service units.

Duties of a social worker in a nursing home generally include the following:

- working with families and hospitals in arranging to have someone admitted
- keeping track of rooms available and length of waiting list, giving tours, and explaining financing
- keeping records of admissions
- working with volunteers
- comforting the dying
- working with a hospice program

- accepting the role of advocacy for residents
- heading the family counsel in the nursing home
- planning and coordinating "family nights" and family care conferences
- acting as the person to whom the residents bring their problems and on whose shoulder they cry

Health Services and Social Concerns

Health-related services outside of an institution are referred to as primary care. Social work has expanded into a variety of health organizations. You may find social workers in free clinics, community mental health centers, union health centers, health maintenance organizations, group medical practices, home health agencies, and industrial settings. Social workers become part of a working team to deal with the medical, social, and psychological aspects of health.

Since the 1960s the field of social work has broadened to include many health related areas. Social workers have a variety of backgrounds in this field. They may be caseworkers, group workers, medical workers, or community organization workers. They work in any area that has social concerns or issues. Some of these include the following:

- home health agencies
- HMOs and other care facilities
- abortion clinics
- adolescent walk-in health centers
- alcohol and chemical dependency centers
- centers for victims of rape and violence
- family planning clinics

- hospices
- neighborhood health centers
- AIDS centers

Social Work in the Home Health Field

Social work in home health services is a large and growing field. The need is greater today because of the push for patients to leave the hospital and care facilities in a much shorter time and because of the growing number of functionally disabled elderly. Discharge planning, community follow-up, and supportive services for home care are becoming an increasingly important part of health care and medical social services.

In January 1986 new codes were accepted by the Health Care Financial Administration (HCFA) to govern Medicare reimbursement to home health agencies for social work. The codes listed five main areas of services that would be covered for payment by Medicare. These areas describe the functions of social workers in home health care.

1. *Assessment of social and emotional factors.* Social workers assess social and emotional factors as they affect the patient's illness, need for care, and response to treatment and adjustment to care. They would also develop a care plan.
2. *Counseling for long-range planning and decision making.* Social workers assess the patient's needs for long-term care, evaluate the home and family situation, and help the patient and his or her family develop an in-home care system. They also explore alternatives to in-home care and arrange for placement.

3. *Community resource planning.* Social workers promote community-centered services, including education, advocacy, and referral.

4. *Short-term therapy.* This area involves goal-oriented intervention in cases of managing terminal illness and reaction/adjustment to such illness, strengthening family/support systems, and resolving conflict related to the lingering illness.

5. *Other.* This area includes other medical social services related to the patient's illness and his or her need for care. Other high-risk indicators may be included that endanger the patient's mental and physical health, including abuse/neglect, inadequate food/medical supplies, or high suicide potential.

HMOs and Preventive and Educational Programs

In 1973 Congress passed legislation that supported Health Maintenance Organizations (HMOs). An HMO is an alternative to third-party insurance coverage. It provides direct medical services for a prearranged fee. Services are provided in a central facility or by independent practitioners. Organization income is limited to membership fees and this limits monies coming in. That becomes a strong incentive to decrease costs by reducing the number and length of hospital stays.

Social workers work with preventive care and health education as well as discharge planning. Clinical social workers provide much of the outpatient psychotherapy staff. They provide the outpatient treatment of patients with mental health problems. This is due partly to the fact that clinical social workers can usually be hired for less money than other mental health professionals with similar psychotherapy skills.

Preventive and educational programs are another exploding area of services. These are services that arise from needs stemming from social problems. Social workers are found working in public health department programs, family planning and health screening, self-help groups, alcohol and drug abuse programs, sex education programs, crisis clinics, rape prevention, and child abuse services. Another fast-growing area of concern and need for services are the victims of AIDS (Acquired Immune Deficiency Syndrome).

Centers and Clinics

Besides preventive and educational programs, there are clinics and centers that deal directly with social health–related issues. Social workers are needed to counsel victims and clients as well as help them work through whatever problems or emergencies they have, evaluate the situation, discuss resources, and help them make necessary choices or decisions.

Social workers in these settings may work through the problem with the client, refer the client to another resource, or help the client get needed health services. Some of these centers or clinics are for a specific need and others are for a specific group of people. Examples include:

• *Abortion clinics.* Services are provided for women seeking to have an abortion to end an unwanted pregnancy. Specific services may include discussing the abortion services and alternatives, referrals, and follow-up counseling services afterward.

• *Adolescent walk-in health centers.* Social services may include evaluating the health problems and concerns of adolescent patients and discussing the impact of the health concerns and possible solutions.

- *Alcohol and chemical dependency centers.* A comprehensive treatment program is provided to patients with alcohol problems and their families. These centers work with social, psychological, spiritual, and physiological factors. Treatment may include lectures, films, reading material, relaxation training, patient group therapy, family group therapy, and one-on-one counseling with both patient and family.

- *Centers for victims of rape and violence.* Social workers in such settings would counsel victims of rape or other violence. They may offer information about sexual assault directly and through community education programs. They may arrange peer counseling and support groups for victims. They are trained advocates. These workers may help the victim go through the examination process and be supportive through any court hearings.

- *Family planning clinics.* Workers in these clinics may discuss pregnancy prevention measures for sexually active people, including birth control alternatives and correct usage of birth control methods. They may also do counseling and referrals for other related health needs.

- *Hospices.* Social workers in a hospice center work with people who are dying and their families. They help them talk out their fears, frustrations, and concerns. They take advantage of other services to make the last days or the time the clients have left as comfortable as possible. Hospice is a concept rather than a setting and may be provided in the clients' homes or in some other setting.

- *Neighborhood health centers.* Services are provided as part of total health care practices. Services depend upon the health problems. Social workers at these settings may also work with educational and preventive programs as well as supportive services.

• *AIDS centers/clinics*. Services in an AIDS clinic may include helping the patient deal with the reality of having the disease. Social workers may counsel with families, friends, and associates. In cases where there is no supportive family member, service workers may also coordinate volunteers needed in supportive services.

Redefining Social Work Health Care

In health care organizations, social work was defined and its expectations were set by others, and the status of social workers was influenced by financing and reimbursement issues. In the 1980s, following a period of professional maturity and development of specialty practices, the role of social workers was changing in the health care field. Social workers took a lead in redefining their roles. Changes included a focus on screening, discharge planning and productivity, abbreviated service modules, and inclusion of the health care institutions in the social workers' advocacy function.

As a profession, health social work is still young, but the distinctive hospital roles are being de-emphasized. Health care reform with managed care eased out the era of specialization. Workers in the "new" health care organization perform many functions that cut across professional boundaries and job classifications.

Even with hospital-based social work practice diminishing, social workers should be aware of other areas such as school-based clinics. They could become part of the program developers and providers of services. School-based clinics offer students opportunities to discuss concerns such as depression, abuse, chemical dependency, and family problems.

Corrections

Social workers in the corrections field usually work as probation or parole officers. They may come from varied backgrounds of specialization in such areas as corrections, human services, and criminal justice. They specialize in direct services for inmates of penal or correctional institutions. They may also help offenders who are eligible for parole to readjust to society. They work with social services, but more closely with law officials and courts. They may have offices in penal institutions, courthouses, private offices, or with county social services.

School Social Work

The changes of the 1960s raised awareness of different groups of their rights to equal opportunities. Also, new interpretations of due process by courts guaranteed the right of every child to an education consistent with his or her needs. This situation created new demands on schools. People entered school social work with backgrounds in casework, group work, clinical, or mental health specialization.

In 1978 the National Association of Social Workers (NASW) published a taxonomy of tasks performed by social workers in schools. There came to be four accepted areas of service in school social work:

1. immediate intervention to reduce stress within or between individuals or groups
2. problem-solving services to pupils, parents, school personnel, or community agencies

3. early identification of students at risk
4. development of coping skills to various groups in school

In 1992 the NASW awarded its newest credential, the "School Social Work Specialist" credential.

Community Organization

Community organization is more of a function than a setting. People come to this type of social work with a background in community organization or group work. A main part of community organization up to the 1950s was fund-raising for the voluntary agencies. Today community organizations are seen as social planners. They emphasize, direct, and influence social change. Some work with health, housing, and transportation. Others work on improving the quality of community living.

Community organizations may use a number of forms of direct action to help people deal with various aspects of their lives. They may research to identify community needs or help draft legislation. They may comment on government proposals in areas like housing, health, and social and welfare services. They may also help organizations in the community work together for social betterment.

Social Settlements

Social settlements differ from other social agencies. The main purpose of settlements is to develop and improve a neighborhood or a cluster of neighborhoods. Settlements are concerned with neighborhood life as a whole rather than just providing selective services. The staff works with individuals, families, or groups. They may use informal counseling and home visiting. They sponsor many activities to help improve or unite neighborhoods through the endeavors of such organizations as friendships clubs, classes, athletic teams, and interest or hobby groups.

Industrial Social Work

During the 1960s occupational social work was popular in Europe. It came to be called "industrial social work" or "personnel assistance" in the United States. Its major growth occurred in the United States in the 1970s. It grew as an extension of the alcohol programs that were being offered to business and industrial workers as employee assistance programs.

In the 1980s industrial social work developed into a specialized area of social work. Services were provided to employee-clients whose personal problems interfered with their job performance. These problems included the following:

- personality conflicts on the job
- family or marital problems that affected the job performance
- alcoholism
- absenteeism
- mental health problems
- physical health problems
- financial problems
- budgetary management difficulties

Because of the growing population of elderly, retirement or pre-retirement planning is another concern and service provided by industrial social workers. Social workers are also employed in corporations and labor unions to provide a variety of work-related services. These areas might include health counseling and preretirement and retirement planning.

Private Practice

Private practice continues to gain professional acceptance in social work. In 1957 NASW acknowledged private practice to be legitimate social work. The NASW Delegate Assembly adopted minimum qualifications in 1962.

The National Federation of Societies of Clinical Social Work promotes private practice and publishes its own journal. Often social workers in private practice are affiliated with medical or psychiatric institutions. They may also be providers of services, and the cost of their services may be reimbursed by insurance coverage. Private practice social workers may work out of their own homes or private offices. Or they may contract out their services to other agencies or to industry.

NASW first published its biennial *NASW Register of Clinical Social Workers* in 1976. This register identifies thousands of "Qualified Clinical Social Workers" who meet NASW standards for clinical practice. In 1986 NASW created the "Diplomate in Clinical Social Work" to distinguish advanced clinical practice expertise.

People who want to go into business for themselves must have at least a master's degree. Some use this as an advancement step. These people will usually be clinical social workers and work in the area of therapy. Many private social workers have to work evenings to meet with clients, attend community meetings, and handle emergency situations.

4

JOBS IN THE PROFESSION

SOCIAL WORKERS INTERACT with individuals, families, and groups. They help people deal with almost any difficulty that they may be having in their lives. The wide scope of problems includes people who are homeless, unemployed, handicapped, seriously ill, or grieving. This "helping profession" has aided the poor, the disadvantaged, and those too young or too old to help themselves.

Social workers help people through counseling services and referral to other sources. They also help make society more responsive to peoples' needs through policy making and advocacy. The major areas where social workers practice include: child welfare and family services, mental health, medical social work, school social work, community organization, planning and policy development, and social welfare administration.

In this chapter we will discuss some of the different types of positions available and some of their duties and qualifications. Eligibility requirements needed for certain jobs may vary between states. Listed are the usual requirements as well as specific duties needed to do the jobs.

Some positions are unique to a particular setting, but similar social work positions can be found in a number of different settings. For instance, a caseworker may be found in a public social service or welfare department, a private social service agency, a hospital, or any number of social organizations. This person may also have responsibilities similar to those of someone working in a different agency and with a different title. As a consequence, it is important in reviewing social work careers to examine the duties and responsibilities of a variety of job titles.

Child Welfare Caseworker

A child welfare caseworker works either with parents who have problems with child rearing or with children who have difficulties in social adjustment. These services are usually referred to as protective services. Child welfare caseworkers investigate homes to protect children from harmful environments. These child protective services may investigate cases of abuse and neglect and intervene as necessary. They study the physical and psychological health of children to determine their needs. Caseworkers may refer children and their parents to appropriate community resources.

Social workers in child welfare services may arrange for adoption and foster care for children. They make sure that needy families are able to give their children proper food, health care, and schooling. They also step in when there is evidence of abuse or neglect. Other services such as the following may be provided by child welfare caseworkers:

- advise parents on the care of severely handicapped infants
- counsel children and youth with social adjustment difficulties
- arrange homemaker services during parent's illness
- start legal action to protect neglected or abused children
- help unmarried parents
- counsel couples on adoption
- evaluate home and parents for possible placement of children for adoption or foster care
- consult with parents, teachers, counselors, and others to help identify problems

Child welfare caseworkers are usually employed in voluntary or public welfare agencies. Child welfare workers also work in residential institutions for children and adolescents. They usually have knowledge and skills in casework methods and have a B.S.W. or M.S.W. degree from a school of social work.

Family Counselor or Family Caseworker

A family counselor or family caseworker works with families having problems in family relationships or other social problems. Family caseworkers do counseling in such areas of family concerns as marriage, parent-child relationships, unwed parents, home management, work adjustment, vocational training, or the need for financial assistance. They may also be involved with the care of the ill, handicapped, or aged, or with helping a family care for members who have physical or mental illness.

Family caseworkers help clients use agency services such as homemaker and day care services, as well as other community resources. They may determine clients' eligibility for financial assistance. They may help travelers, runaways, or other people having difficulties in achieving stability.

To do their job, the social workers may counsel individuals. Their goals may be to strengthen personal or family relationships or help clients cope with problems. They may also provide information and referral (I&R) services for family budgeting, money management, locating housing, securing homemaker's services, finding assistance for elderly, job training, and day care. Some social workers may specialize in adult protection services. They intervene in cases of battered wives, neglected or abused elderly, or mentally impaired individuals.

Family caseworkers may work in public assistance and other agencies such as family services, Travelers Aid, and American Red Cross Home Services. They usually must have the skills and knowledge of casework methods and a B.S.W. or M.S.W. from a school of social work.

Social Service Caseworker

A social service caseworker (also called community placement worker, intake worker, or social service worker) counsels and helps individuals and families requiring assistance from a social service agency. The caseworker interviews clients with problems such as personal and family adjustments, finances, employment, and physical or mental impairment, to determine the nature and degree of problems.

The caseworker gathers physical, psychological, and social information. These factors are evaluated to determine the clients' situations and capacities. Clients may be counseled privately, with their families, or in groups. Referrals may be made to community resources. Social service caseworkers must keep records, and they may determine eligibility for financial assistance. They also may work with professionals in other agencies.

Case Aide or Eligibility Worker

A case aide works on similar aspects of cases as caseworkers or provides services to less complex cases. Case aides work under the close and regular supervision of a caseworker. Their qualifications may vary from a high school degree, related experience, associate degree, or bachelor's degree.

An eligibility worker interviews applicants or recipients to determine eligibility for public assistance. Eligibility workers may interpret and explain rules and regulations governing eligibility and grants, method of payment, and legal rights to applicants or recipients. They also may keep records of personal and financial data obtained from applicants or recipients. In their evaluations they may determine initial or continuing eligibility.

Eligibility workers help determine whether applicants are eligible for various public welfare, employment, and medical assistance programs. Then they authorize the amount of money payment, food stamps, medical care, or other general assistance. They may identify the need for and refer applicants to social services and other agencies and community resources. They are responsible for written reports and submit recommendations for their supervisor to consider. They prepare and keep records of assigned cases. Qualifications for eligibility workers may be similar to those of case aides.

Casework Supervisor

A casework supervisor supervises social service agency staff, volunteers, and students of schools of social work and coordinates their activities. Supervisors assign caseloads and related duties. They coordinate activities of staff in providing counseling to transients and other clients with emergencies.

They may assist agency staff through conferences in analyzing case problems and in improving their diagnostic and helping skills. They also evaluate staff performances and recommend any needed actions. Supervisors help develop and implement agency administration policy. They may also conduct or direct staff development. Usually a supervisor will have a master's degree from a school of social work. Supervisory positions are seen as promotional and are usually based on education and experience in the field.

Social Welfare Administrator/Director

A social welfare administrator/director directs the agency or the major function of a public or voluntary organization that provides services in the social welfare field. The administrator works with a board of directors and committees to establish policies and programs and then administers these programs. This person may also determine policies and define the scope of services within the regulations if the agency is functioning without a board of directors.

Directors may develop and administer standards and procedures related to personnel. They do staff development, establish a budget, and manage the physical facilities. They may interpret agency purpose and programs to the community. Responsibilities may also include establishing and maintaining relationships with other agencies. They organize and meet the community needs and services. They may also direct or coordinate fund-raising, public relations, and fact-finding or research activities.

Administrators or directors are employed in such settings as child support enforcement programs, child welfare, community welfare councils, family casework, youth service agencies, health organizations, and information education and recreation. They are also found in public welfare and fund-raising organizations. Qualifications may vary with the agency. Experience in the field is usually required, as is training or experience in public administration or administration of programs.

Psychiatric Social Worker

A psychiatric social worker usually works in a hospital, clinic, or mental health center. These workers help patients respond to their treatment and form a link with family and the community. They may investigate case situations and present information to psychiatrists and clinical psychologists. They may also consult with psychiatrists in direct treatment with patients. They help patients respond to treatment and assist in adjustment leading to and following discharge. They also may interpret psychiatric treatment to the patient's family.

Psychiatric social workers are also employed in state mental hospitals, Veterans Administration hospitals, for-profit psychiatric hospitals, substance abuse treatment facilities, and psychiatric units of general hospitals. They provide individual and group therapy for psychiatric patients. They also serve as a link between patient, psychiatric agency, and community. Psychiatric social workers may refer the patient or patient's family to other community resources. They are usually required to have the knowledge and skills of casework methods from a school of social work.

Clinical Social Worker, Private Practice

This growing group of mental health workers offers psychotherapy or counseling to individual families or groups. These social workers counsel families of troubled adolescents and people with marital problems, assist individuals with job stress, or set up support groups for persons with special health problems such as cancer.

Some private practitioners specialize in organized consulting and contract with employers to do employee assistance as an industrial or occupational social worker. Others provide consultant services to trade unions and develop educational, recreational, and service programs for active and retired members.

A growing segment of private practice social workers specializes in gerontological services. Some run support groups for family caretakers or for adult children of aging parents. Geriatric case management services on a fee-for-service basis may also be offered. They may assess service needs and advise the elderly or family members about choices in such services as housing, transportation, and long-term care. They may just monitor or coordinate the services, depending upon the amount of services required from the family.

Gerontological social workers often serve as consultants for governmental agencies, community organizations, and business firms. They might evaluate existing programs for the elderly, advising on new programs and services.

Private practice offers variety, prestige, and the potential for higher pay. Social workers consider private practice a way to advance professionally without becoming a supervisor or a director. Some private practitioners specialize in organizational consulting. In addition to the M.S.W. degree, private practitioners also need a well-rounded work experience to develop a network of contacts for referral purposes. Being a good entrepreneur is important for success in this rapidly developing but highly competitive field.

Clinical social workers play a vital role in providing mental health services in all types of health delivery systems. Clinical social workers provide psychotherapy and consultation services in the private sector on a fee basis. They also serve as salaried psychotherapists, counselors, and consultants in organizational settings, such as hospitals and clinics. They may work out of their own homes or set up private offices.

Medical/Hospital Social Worker

Social workers who are employed in hospitals and other health care establishments such as clinics, rehabilitation centers, drug and alcohol abuse centers, or related establishments are often called medical social workers. They aid patients and their families with personal difficulties that are associated with illnesses or that are interfering with treatment. Medical social workers work closely with physicians and other medical workers. They help to further the understanding of the patients' social and emotional factors as they relate to health problems. Those who work in nursing homes may help with the admissions process and direct the activities program in addition to counseling residents and families. These social workers help families and patients understand, accept, and follow through with medical plans. They provide services to help patients achieve as much health and social adjustment as the patient is capable of achieving. They use resources such as other agencies to assist patients to resume life in the community or to learn to live with their disabilities.

They also may help plan for the improvement of health services by interpreting social factors important to the development of programs. They provide supervision and direction to workers engaged in clinics and in home services program activities. Social workers in the home health field work with evaluation, assessment, and case management. They also do some administrative and supervisory work.

Medical social workers are employed in general hospitals, clinics, rehabilitation centers, or in related programs. They may be employed as consultants in other agencies. In most cases, they are required to have at least an M.S.W.

Hospital social workers play a major role in direct care functions in the pediatric or obstetric departments of a hospital. Hospital social workers may also work directly with patients and families of patients suffering from emotional illnesses. They may help organize health screening and health education programs. They may collaborate with community agencies to coordinate care or coordinate employee assistance programs. Included in hospitals' efforts to bring in more business, social workers may offer new services, such as adult day care, respite care, hospice care, health screening, and education and work-site wellness.

In these settings the workers may provide information about sociological or economic backgrounds of patients for doctors. These backgrounds might include problems of inadequate housing, lack of money for medicine, and other concerns that may affect or cause problems with the illness. They may also be involved in discharge planning, that is, they may counsel those who are being discharged or work with other agencies to help the patients return to everyday life. Many specialize in such areas as care for the dying and for victims of certain diseases, and maternal and child care. Their responsibilities may include:

- taking financial or social histories
- consulting with medical staff on the psychosocial concerns
- counseling hospital patients
- advising family on care or treatment
- suggesting home care arrangements after discharge
- helping patients and families cope with illness, recovery, and rehabilitation

An increasing role for hospital social workers is to assist the family caregivers. This includes taking the lead in organizing support groups for families of patients suffering from cancer, Alzheimer's disease, or other illnesses that impose a heavy burden on families.

Discharge planning has become an important area of practice for workers because of prospective payment. Medicare has a new system of paying hospital care that makes timely discharge financially beneficial. Discharge plans include such services as meals-on-wheels to oxygen equipment or at-home nursing follow-up. Qualifications are similar to those for medical social workers.

School Social Worker

A school social worker may be found in any school—from nursery through college. School social workers are also known as home and school visitors, school adjustment counselors, and visiting teachers. These workers help children when they are having difficulties adapting to school life or when some professional help is indicated. They may also work in special schools for the emotionally disturbed and the handicapped. They help with vocational counseling and personal problems at the higher levels.

They also work with students with learning difficulties to help them fulfill maximum potential. They counsel children whose behavior or school progress indicates the need for individual guidance. They consult with parents, teachers, and other school personnel to determine causes of problems and to find solutions.

School social workers may arrange for medical, psychiatric, and other examinations that might help determine the causes of difficulties in school. They may also work with parents' or teachers' attitudes that may have caused or aggravated problems. A change of class or school, special tutoring, or other treatment may be recommended to help students work out their problems.

In the educational setting, social work goals support basic educational goals. Social workers in schools can help children benefit from basic instruction. They may work with schools to help develop the personal and social competencies necessary for learning. They focus on students' abilities to fully use the educational opportunities. They will also intervene in order to improve conditions in a school or community that will help a child's development.

School social workers may also serve as a liaison between school and community resources, such as family service agencies, child guidance clinics, protective services, doctors, and ministers. They serve as consultants to school personnel in respect to children or situations that are not referred for direct services. They usually are required to have the knowledge and skills in casework methods acquired through working on degrees in school social work.

Industrial Social Worker

Industrial social workers make up one of the newest fields of social work. These workers often work in employee assistance programs. Industrial social work is sometimes called occupational social work or personal assistance. Industrial social work provides a social service to employees whose personal problems are interfering with their job performance. Social workers deal with a wide variety of problems:

- personality problems that interfere with relations with management or coworkers
- marital difficulties
- parent-child problems at home
- alcoholism
- absenteeism
- mental and physical health problems
- financial and budget management

Referrals are made to the industrial social worker from management or directly from the employees themselves. Services usually consist of brief social work intervention. Those needing long-term services are referred to appropriate community services.

Industrial social workers may also consult with supervisors and with management. Management may seek these services to avoid or solve problems without the need to refer the employee. These services are usually offered through the personnel department or health unit.

Social Group Worker

Social group worker is defined as a goal-directed activity with small groups of people meeting their social and emotional needs. Groups may focus on tasks or treatment. The task goals are directed to the individual's needs in the group as a whole. Treatment may emphasize one or a combination of goals: educational, growth, remediation, socialization, or the self-help group.

Social group workers operate on the theory that social groups could support individuals and solve social problems. They have set up their practices after the model of social casework. Social group work has become more clinical. It stresses education for citizenship and development of socialization rather than any treatment of social illnesses.

Social group work is associated with schools of progressive education. They are concerned mainly with how social groups, such as the family, peer groups, social clubs, and community groups, affect individuals' socialization and social development.

Group workers are found in community centers, neighborhood or settlement houses, hospitals, institutions for children or the aged, youth centers, and housing projects. They perform a wide range of services depending upon where they are employed and whom they serve. Some of their duties might include:

- organize groups for senior citizens, children, and teens
- develop recreational, physical education, or cultural programs
- instruct participants in activities such as sports, group dances, games, arts, crafts, and dramatics
- organize current events and discussion groups
- conduct consumer problem surveys
- perform similar activities to stimulate an interest in civic responsibility

Group workers promote the group work concept to help members develop their own activities. Workers may consult with other community resources regarding specific individuals and make referrals. They are usually required to have skills gained through a degree program at a school of social work.

Program Aide in Group Work

An aide may lead informal group work activities as directed by agency program staff. Aides receive instruction from a group worker before starting any therapeutic group activities. Aides may plan program details to meet needs and interests of individual members. They may interest participants in various activities, such as arts and crafts and dramatics. They work to help develop new skills and interests. They may demonstrate techniques for active sports, group dances, and games. They may also work with part-time or volunteer staff. Program aides are employed in social service agencies, such as community centers, neighborhood houses, settlement houses, and hospitals.

Tenant Relations Coordinator

A management aide helps residents of public and private housing projects and apartments in relocation. Aides may also provide information concerning regulations, facilities, and services. They explain rules established by the owner or management. These rules might deal with sanitation, maintenance, or parking requirements. They may also inform tenants of facilities such as laundries and playgrounds. They advise homemakers needing assistance in child care, food, money management, and housekeeping problems. Aides also explain services and the location of community services, such as clinics and recreation programs. They keep records and prepare reports for owners or management.

Community Organization Worker

Although community organizers also set up their practice after the model of social casework, their focus differs from social group workers. Social group workers focus on clinical approaches; community organizers focus on intergroup processes and healthy social relationships.

Community organization workers plan, organize, and work with community groups concerned with social problems of the community. They may work to stimulate, promote, and coordinate agencies, groups, and individuals to meet identified needs. They study and assess the strengths and weaknesses of existing resources. They also interpret needs, programs, and services for the agencies, groups, and individuals involved. They provide leadership and assistance as needed. Other duties may be to prepare reports, assist in budget preparation, and assist in fund-raising.

Community organization workers may work in specialized fields such as:

- aging
- juvenile delinquency
- urban renewal and development
- mental and physical health
- public or voluntary coordinating agency
- community welfare or health council
- combined fund-raising and welfare planning

They usually need a degree from a school of social work.

Parole Officer

Parole officers work with juveniles or adult offenders from correctional institutions. They are involved with activities related to the conditional release of these offenders. They establish a relationship with the offenders. They also must become familiar with the offenders' social history before and during institutionalization. They help develop a release plan. Parole officers provide a program of supervised treatment and interviews. They can help the parolee secure necessary education or employment.

The goals in corrections are the prevention of crime and rehabilitation of criminals. Priority is given to such preventive services as tutoring and recreation, especially for juveniles. Correction officers may provide the following services: counseling juveniles or adults; helping offenders readjust to society; intervening in problems that come up because of the return to home or community; and helping offenders secure necessary education, employment, or community service. The parole officer may refer parolees to social resources in the community that aid in rehabilitation. Attempts are made to involve the families of parolees to help in the adjustment process. Evaluations of a parolee's progress are done on a follow-up basis. The officer may return the parolee to an institution or arrange appropriate disciplinary action by the paroling authority where necessary. Parole officers are usually employed by correctional institutions or parole agencies. They are usually required to have knowledge and skills in casework methods acquired through a degree program at a school of social work.

Probation Officer

Probation officers work with juvenile or adult offenders. They help determine which juvenile cases fall within the jurisdiction of the court and which should be adjusted informally or referred to other agencies. They may release children to parents or other authorities pending a hearing. The officers may conduct prehearing or presentence investigations of adults and juveniles by interviewing the offender, his or her family, and others concerned. They also prepare social histories for courts, interpret findings, and suggest plans of treatment.

Probation officers arrange for placement or clinical services if ordered by the court. They work with an offender on probation according to a treatment plan aimed at discharge from probation. Evaluations are done on a follow-up basis. Disciplinary action is secured, if necessary, from the court. Probation officers may be administratively attached to the court or to a separate agency serving the court. Officers are usually required to have knowledge and skills in casework methods gained through a degree program at a school of social work.

5

Prospects in the Social Work Field

Whenever there are social changes or social problems, social workers are needed to help people deal with these changes or concerns. There have been some changes and trends lately that will affect the future of social workers. Some of these changes and trends will also affect working conditions and problems that social workers will be facing.

The Shifting Family Structure

At the passage of the Social Security Act of 1935, a typical family included a mother as a homemaker, a father as a breadwinner, three children, and a marriage for life. In 1990 only 13 percent of families had this definition. There has been an increase in singles, unmarried women having children, divorce, and desertion. The average size of the U.S. household decreased about 12 percent in the thirty years from 1970 to 2000.

By 1990 half of all Americans had no child-rearing responsibilities; other families had three, four, or five children. Eighty percent of children were supported by 30 percent of the population. Unfortunately, people who don't have children are less likely to support family issues. Already this is demonstrated in a reluctance to support public education.

Two other changes in the family structure are shaping social concerns today. In 1960 about 30 percent of women were working outside the home. In 2002 this number increased to roughly 65 percent. In 1935 only 6 percent of the population was sixty-five years or older; in 1990 it was 12 percent, and by 2030 it is estimated to be 23 percent of the population.

Social workers are taking an increased role in important reform issues such as family preservation and health care. On the back side of that, social workers will have to increasingly work with children who get into trouble or have problems and help the elderly cope with obstacles in life.

Medical Waivers

There is also a trend to keep the elderly in their homes as long as is feasible with the support of homemakers' assistance and home health aides. This trend was made possible with the financial help of medical waivers. This is also true for the chronically ill and others who could stay home if they had outside help, rather than enter nursing homes or other medical facilities. This trend is also directly influenced by the concerns for cost-effective programs. Approximately 50 to 60 percent of all nursing home beds are paid for by welfare. With the trend toward cost effectiveness, there is an increased need for public agencies to case manage such services as homemakers', home health aides, and other supportive services.

Deinstitutionalization

In the 1960s there was a push to get people out of permanent and long-term care in state hospitals and other treatment centers. The push led to group homes and residential treatment centers. Today this push is becoming even stronger. The efforts now are to get people out of group homes and into private home care or to keep people out of institutional treatment altogether by means of outpatient care.

This push was increased with the concern for the cost effectiveness of care; this approach looks at how much care costs rather than the quality of care provided to clients. For example, if it costs $150 a day for care in a state hospital, the care in the community could drop to $62 a day. Consequently the goal is to get more people out of long-term treatment. Social workers are needed for local case management, follow-up, and supervision of the caregivers of these people.

Case Management

Social workers have worked with some case management for years. But with deinstitutionalization and with cutting back on long-term care, three main groups of people—as identified by the NASW in its pamphlet on *Standards and Guidelines for Social Work Case Management for the Functionally Impaired*—will need some type of case management:

1. the frail and functionally impaired elderly
2. vocational rehabilitation clientele
3. deinstitutionalized state hospital patients

Case management is a function of social work. It is the management of a client's needs. The process of case management means those social workers:

- identify the needs of the client
- identify available resources
- develop a plan of care
- coordinate services
- monitor services and care
- evaluate services
- act as an advocate for the client

Homeless Population

Because of some of these other trends, the number of the homeless has increased. Patients who were committed to state mental hospitals are being put out of institutions much sooner. Some of these people are ending up on the streets. They include the chronically chemically dependent and the mentally ill. The IQ level for eligibility for medical waivers for services was lowered from the marginal level of 85 to 70. This meant that lower-functioning people with IQs between 70 and 85 were no longer eligible for services. In today's sophisticated world, people who function at lower levels will increasingly need help dealing with employment and everyday living skills. The U.S. Bureau of the Census estimated that there were 228,621 homeless people in 1990. However, the

National Alliance to End Homelessness estimated that there were 750,000 homeless people. The question is, do people in shelters count as being homeless?

Acquired Immune Deficiency Syndrome (AIDS)

AIDS is killing people. It causes tremendous medical, economic, social, and emotional burdens both on people with AIDS and on their families and friends. In many cases, people with AIDS often die within three to five years of contracting the disease. In addition to the suffering of the victims themselves, they leave survivors to grieve and suffer from the loss.

The AIDS statistics—as reported by the Centers for Disease Control (CDC)—are staggering. These figures include both adults and children:

- At the end of 1982 approximately 1,000 cases were reported.
- At the end of 1984 approximately 9,000 cases were reported.
- At the end of 1994 approximately 80,600 cases were reported.
- At the end of 2000 approximately 125,000 cases were reported.

Data from the HIV/AIDS surveillance (U.S. Department of Health and Human Service Center for Disease Control, 2000) give these staggering numbers. Eighty-six percent of all AIDS cases have been reported in metropolitan areas, although only 75 percent of the population live in these areas. In January 2000 the CDC reported that AIDS is the leading killer of Americans ages twenty-five to forty-four. Today 82 percent of AIDS cases in the United States were transmitted through one of the following ways:

- 46 percent between homosexuals/bisexuals
- 25 percent between intravenous drug users
- 11 percent between heterosexuals

Information as well as materials to help prevent AIDS needs to be continually developed and distributed to people. Avoiding the behaviors that place people at risk could almost stop AIDS; however, behaviors are hard to change. Other problems and concerns related to AIDS include the high cost of AIDS drugs, AIDS testing, gay issues, discrimination, health needs, pre- and post-test counseling, help to apply for insurance or Social Security benefits, and hospice care.

As more and more social workers have contact with people with AIDS, they will have to be involved with social policy. To be effective in policy formation and be able to offer service, social workers need to be familiar with a wide array of issues and legal matters such as:

- client involvement with AIDS research
- privacy and confidentiality
- mandatory screening and testing
- access to health insurance
- getting professional services

Social workers who understand the legal issues of AIDS can increase their ability to work toward changing legislation and to advocate for their clients.

Child Abuse

Nearly four children die each day from abuse or neglect. In 1998, 2,972,862 children were reported abused or neglected (U.S. Department of Health and Human Services, National Center on Child Abuse and Neglect). For those who do live, their lives will be affected. Many people who were abused as children turn to crime and violence themselves.

Child abuse and neglect include a wide range of behaviors and family problems. Physical child abuse means that some physical damage is done to a child. Child neglect means that a child is denied some of the basic necessities of life, such as proper food, shelter, medical care, clothing, and education. Sexual abuse occurs when some adult responsible for the care of the child becomes involved in improper sexual activities with that child. Emotional abuse may include verbally attacking a child or the denial of the love and attention that all children need to grow and develop.

The National Clearinghouse on Child Abuse and Neglect Information is a national resource for service providers and local, state, and national agencies, both public and private. Members of Congress, researchers, and concerned members of the general public also use it. For a current catalog of publications and services, contact:

National Clearinghouse on Child Abuse and Neglect Information
330 C Street SW
Washington, D.C. 20047
(800) 394-3366
calib.com/nccanch

Networking

Helping and serving people in today's world is not as simple as giving out a little food, helping with rent payments, or talking out problems. As life has become more complex, the resources and services available to meet these needs have also become complex. One agency cannot be on top of or be the expert in all aspects of the helping field. Instead of doing it all themselves, social workers need to learn what resources are available and network or connect the need with the services available. This is especially true in the field of social welfare but also in all other fields of practice.

Case management is coordinating and overseeing services for clients who cannot manage this responsibility for themselves. Networking is coordinating services and resources for clients, other professionals, or agencies. There are four main types of networking. The first two are also used in case management.

1. The natural support system involves professional intervention to help clients connect to family, friends, or colleagues.
2. Client-agency linkage is professional intervention to help link the client to another professional service or another agency in the community.
3. Interprofessional linkages involve linking professionals to other professionals to help meet the agency goals.
4. Human service organization networking links the services and cooperation of agencies through ties established by top-level administration.

Unfortunately there is often professional jealousy between agencies. In those cases networking becomes guarded and untrusting—

if tried at all. Sometimes agencies don't want to share the responsibilities of providing services with other agencies. Sometimes when funding is low, some agencies don't want the responsibility of providing services for a plan that they didn't initiate.

The process of networking can be set up in a manner similar to case management. Instead of case management, a professional in an agency initiates or oversees services or resources management. The networking process can imitate, and has successfully imitated, the case management process:

- identify the need of a client or the agency
- identify available resources from other agencies
- develop cooperation/referrals between agencies
- coordinate resources between agencies and professionals
- periodically evaluate the use of resources
- be an advocate for your own agency or services

Personal Values and Beliefs

Social workers are put in the position of working with social concerns or problems that may conflict with their own personal values or beliefs. Objectivity is important for social workers who work with many different types of people, problems, and issues. Can or even should social workers remain totally objective in dealing with issues that they personally may object to, such as abortion, severe behavior control methods, forced sterilization of mentally impaired females, the right to die, or the use of psychotropic medications?

Should social workers have the right to state personal beliefs? Should they just learn to ignore or deal with their feelings? Do they have the right to choose what service to offer and refuse to consider others? Should a social worker choose the field of practice or the type of setting more carefully? These are questions that all social workers have to face and deal with individually.

Some associations or concerned organizations may help find possible solutions. The administration in some agencies will allow staff to refer such services to others who will perform the services. Sometimes you may be able to offer alternatives. Suppose a client wants an abortion (if it is legal) and you explore other alternatives like foster care, adoption, and unwed services. What alternative do you have if the client still insists on exploring abortion and you can't morally accept it?

Some agencies will allow you to refer this client to another agency or to another staff member in your own agency rather than have you go against your beliefs. But this would have to be a service that is not a major part of your job or stressed in your job description. You have to use some judgment in choosing where you want to work. If you object to abortion, and refuse to discuss it, a family planning agency is not the type of agency for you to work in.

Professional Overlapping

The issues and social concerns of social workers overlap with those of other professionals. This overlapping is sometimes a problem for social workers. For example, a hospital administrator may hire a nurse to coordinate home health care and discharge planning. But a hospital social worker may perform the same tasks. A high school counselor may talk to troubled teens, or a school social worker may work with them. Administrators may choose one professional over another because of past experience and knowledge of that profession. Or by looking at cost effectiveness, they may decide to hire someone at a lower salary.

Job Outlook

Through the year 2010, employment in social work is expected to increase faster than the average for most occupations. This trend is partially due to the increasing population of the elderly. According to the *Occupational Outlook Handbook*, this growth in employment will vary depending upon funding and public, private, and third-party spending for social work services. The main source of openings will be to replace those who quit working or change jobs.

Public Agencies

Job growth in public agencies will continue to vary in different regions. Despite regional variations, state and local governments are expected to retain their importance as leading employers of social workers. Declassification—making B.S.W.s eligible for jobs that only M.S.W.s could apply for before—may lessen the demand for M.S.W.s in public agencies.

Schools

Expansion has already occurred in elementary and secondary schools because of the Education for All Handicapped Children Act of 1975. The overall outlook for school social workers is good, especially for persons with training or experience in this area. The availability of state and local funding will dictate the actual increase in jobs in this setting.

Hospitals

Hospitals now provide one out of ten social work jobs. Because of the anticipated slowdown in hospital growth, increased jobs in this setting are unlikely. Financial and organizational changes will affect hospital social work. Discharge planning will become very important and familiarity with community agencies and organizations will be important for prospective social workers in this setting. Prospects for hospital social workers should be favorable through the year 2010.

Home Health

Home health will be a growing area of practice for two main reasons: hospitals are shortening the stay of patients, and the population and needs of the elderly are growing. In some situations, social workers will be needed to evaluate, assess, and manage cases. In others, administrative and supervisory duties will be needed.

Outpatient Facilities

HMOs (Health Maintenance Organizations) and rehabilitation facilities that offer alcohol and drug abuse programs will be among the outpatient facilities that will be growing and needing to fill social work positions. Funding is not a problem in these areas. HMOs offer comprehensive care for a preestablished fee. The employer or insurance often covers alcohol and drug rehabilitation programs.

In HMOs, social work may provide counseling in teenage pregnancy, stress management, substance abuse, abortion, crisis intervention for spouse/child abuse, assistance for the elderly, and case management.

Private Practice

Expansion is expected in private practice. But private practice doesn't guarantee success. Private practitioners must be able to market themselves and compete with psychologists, psychiatric nurses, counselors, and other mental health providers. This is helped by the growing acceptance of private practice social work by the profession and by the public. Health insurance availability and an affluent population willing to pay for services for personal problems will help provide funding sources. A growing program in employee assistance may contract for more services and will also help. Social workers may run training sessions on group dynamics or counsel employees on a variety of problems.

Other Variables

Opportunities for social work positions will greatly depend upon a number of factors:

- academic credentials
- experience
- field of practice
- geographic location
- competition
- supply and demand

Earnings

Salaries vary greatly depending on location, field of practice, and the type of agency. It is also important whether the agency is public or private. Greatest earnings will be for private practitioners, administrators, teachers, and researchers. According to the U.S. Department of Labor, average annual earnings of child, family, and school social workers were $31,470 in 2000.

Median annual earnings in the industries employing the largest numbers of child, family, and school social workers in 2000 were: local government, except education and hospitals, $33,950; hospitals, $33,150; health and allied services, $28,270; individual and family services, $28,160; and residential care, $26,620.

Career Advancement

Advancement in social work usually comes in the form of promotion to supervisor, administrator, or director. Like administrators, directors hire, train, and supervise staff; develop and evaluate agency programs; make budget decisions; solicit funds; and represent the agency in public. Becoming a director may be a promotion, but it is getting out of the realm of direct social work.

Private Practice

Private practice offers variety, prestige, and potential for higher pay. Private practice is one way for social workers to advance professionally without becoming a supervisor or a director. Some private practitioners counsel individuals or groups. Others specialize in organizational consulting. They need at least an M.S.W. degree and a network of contacts for referrals of clients. Being a good entrepreneur is important for success in this highly competitive field.

Agency Advancement

There are advancements in some agencies through years of experience, additional education, testing, or a combination of these. An example of such advancement would be a social worker with a B.S.W. entering the agency at a Social Worker I level. A social worker with at least two years' experience and who has passed a test may qualify for a Social Worker II level. To become a Social Worker III, a social worker would have to have an M.S.W. This might allow for additional responsibility and for moving into a higher wage scale. Once a person with a master's degree reaches the top of the scale, he or she would have to look at other options.

Licensing

As of January 1995 all fifty states have registration or licensure and thirty-three have vendorship laws. The National Association of Social Workers (NASW) offers voluntary certification. It awards the title ACSW (Academy of Certified Social Workers) to those who qualify. It is going to be more and more important in the future to be licensed, certified, or registered. The country is going toward requiring more qualifications. Because an increasing number of social workers have these qualifications, it is easier to make them mandatory.

Working Conditions

Most social workers are employed for thirty-five to forty hours over a five-day week. Many social workers employed at private agencies work part-time. Many social workers have to work evenings and some weekends to meet clients, attend community meetings, and handle emergency situations. Extra leave is usually granted for overtime. Some travel is necessary to visit clients and to attend meetings and workshops.

Paperwork/Stress

People seek social work careers because they want to work with people. Unfortunately in some settings, on the average, only one-fourth of the time is spent with clients. The rest of the time is devoted to paperwork resulting from large caseloads. This is particularly true in public agencies and varies between different settings.

Stress often is joined with enormous problems and conflicting demands from courts, police, clients, social agencies, and community members. Emotional burnout may come with the dual expenditure of physical and emotional caring spread between home and work. Attitudes and goals of management also bring stress. Management is trained to think in terms of productivity and outcomes rather than in terms of individual needs and concerns.

Liability

In recent years social workers have been given administrative reprimands and have been fired, downgraded, or reassigned for allegedly mishandling their cases. Hundreds of workers and agencies have been charged with professional malpractice or violation of clients' rights. Claims range from a few thousand to millions of dollars.

Criminal prosecution is also increasing. Some social workers have been indicted for official malfeasance or negligent homicide. Others have been brought before grand jury investigations. Legal actions have been taken mainly against child protection units.

Legal action against social workers can provoke anxiety, even if the majority of cases don't come to trial. The best legal liability protection comes from professional expertise, keeping within social work ethics and values, and understanding legal grounds. You can help protect yourself in the following ways:

- Know your legal responsibilities.
- Document cases.
- Know your agency's policies and procedures.
- Check your agency's liability coverage.
- Consider liability coverage for yourself.
- Join national associations.

Violence Against Social Workers

Physical and emotional violence is increasing against social workers in all settings. The increase of violence is partially blamed on:

- the deinstitutionalization movement
- discharged patients refusing psychotropic drugs (drugs that act on the mind)
- the right to refuse treatment
- adult and child protection intervention
- new intervention in roles of domestic violence
- child support enforcement
- abortion clinics
- welfare fraud investigation

Training programs are needed to help recognize events that lead up to client violence. Also, social workers need to become aware of safe physical and management techniques for protecting themselves and their clients. Some suggested safeguards for those who deal with violence are to establish an electronic emergency signaling system—two-way radios in automobiles for home visits and transporting clients—and to use a buddy system.

Additional Social Concerns

Other areas in which social workers will be needed include:

- housing problems
- health care
- programs to protect against abuse of children, women, and the elderly
- aid to the mentally ill
- control of substance abuse

To be the most effective in these and other areas of concern, at some time social workers will need additional training, experience, or education. Graduate certification in special areas such as gerontology is one possibility. Competition is tough, and to be competitive, you have to be the best person for the job!

6

SETTING PERSONAL GOALS

IDENTIFYING YOUR INTERESTS, abilities, likes, and dislikes can help you make decisions concerning work. This is important because a career such as social work affects more than just money and working conditions. You are deciding on a specific lifestyle. When you make a career choice, you also decide:

- what types of people you will work with
- how much leisure time you will have
- where you will live and work
- amount of job security
- level of earnings

Evaluating Career Goals

What type of career in social work do you want? Who do you want to work with? What type of problems do you want to be involved with? What kind of setting is appealing to you? These and the questions below are only to get you thinking. The following lists of possible answers to the questions aren't meant to include every setting or every job. They are only meant to suggest general categories. The questions may help you narrow possibilities.

What kind of people interest you? Who would you want to work with?

Youth

child protection social services
correctional programs for youth
neighborhood centers
school social work
clinical social work specializing in children
hospital social work with youth programs
social or recreation programs

Elderly

nursing home social work
services for the aging in county welfare
family social services for the aging
community programs for the aging
hospital social services specializing in the aged
home health programs
nutritional programs
senior citizens' centers
adult protection programs in social services

Families

family social services
mental health therapy groups
community action programs

clinical social work, family practice
county welfare departments with Aid to Families with
Dependent Children (AFDC)

Other adults
corrections, adult parole or probation
clinical social work
industrial social work
mental health centers

What kind of problems do you want to work with?

Health problems
drug and alcohol treatment programs
medical services in family social services
hospital social services
hospice programs
nursing home social services
home health programs

Mental health/behavior problems/stress
correctional facilities
mental health centers/programs
school social work
industrial social work
private practice
school social work

Intervention/protection
county child or adult protection units
welfare departments

family social services
mental health programs

Recreational/social programs
neighborhood centers
nutritional programs
senior citizens' centers
settlement houses
community action groups

Narrowing Your Choices

Whether you are still in high school, in college, want to change careers, or just want to get back into the workforce, you like or dislike a variety of things. These likes and dislikes should influence your choice of career. Evaluate who you are, what you find interesting, what jobs you have undertaken, your personality, and what you like to do.

A professional in one field of practice in social work may need to have different interests, concerns, and abilities than a professional in another. A probation officer and a nursing home social worker may not share the same personal qualifications. In fact, a nursing home social worker may find more in common with a hospital social worker and have similar qualities. A probation officer and a school social worker may have similar interests and concerns.

In evaluating yourself, think about some of the choices you have already made:

- What courses did you like in school? In community classes?
- What duties did you like in a previous job? In volunteer work?

- What things do you enjoy in your hobbies? In leisure activities?
- What personality qualities do you see in yourself? Do others see in you?

Compare what you like and what you dislike with the roles and duties of different settings and jobs. You could find yourself narrowing your scope of interest in the field. You may change as you mature and gain experience and exposure in the field. You may find yourself not wanting to narrow the field of choices . . . yet. Or you may know exactly what field of practice you want to go into. The important thing to remember is that your choice is important. Base it on who you are, what is important to you, and the kinds of things you want to be doing.

Improving Your Marketability

Many accredited bachelor's degree programs do not require a minor. However, to increase your job possibilities, consider getting minors in your areas of interest. Criminal justice and/or chemical dependency combination minors may greatly increase your chances of getting a job, if these are in your area of interest. Concentrating in gerontology at the four-year degree level may open doors in many new fields with the aging. A psychology minor may be a good introduction to a master's or doctorate program or help prepare you for many entry-level jobs in the mental health setting.

Your focus or direction should depend upon your interests and what type of job you want when you graduate. When looking into any two-year, four-year, master's, or Ph.D. programs, look at the specialization of the courses. Also look at what concentration and/or minors you can combine with your basic program. A person graduating with a B.S.W. and a minor in a specialization will be more desirable for a job position than a person coming out with only a B.S.W.

Don't forget to look for educational programs that give you enough opportunity for field practice, volunteering, internships, and other work experiences. Any work-related experience—paid or unpaid—can be put on a résumé. Getting actual work experience while still in school looks great on applications. But perhaps even more important, this experience will help you decide if that particular setting or job is for you—or even if social work is for you.

Education

Most social work positions demand a four-year degree in social work, sociology, or psychology. Many professional associations require an individual to have a degree from an accredited program in social work to be certified. You may have a high standing in graduate school with a B.S.W. from an accredited program. Most clinical social work positions in VA hospitals and mental health centers as well as requirements for private practice look for a master's degree or more. For teaching or research you may need a doctorate degree.

Social work aides or technicians are social-work supportive or paraprofessional positions. Sometimes work experience, previous jobs, passing a test, or an interview may qualify aides. Technicians usually are graduates from a two-year community college in a human service program. They also may have related training or backgrounds.

Find out what your individual state or agency requires in terms of education, licensing, registration, or training. To find out that information, you can review a number of sources:

- Communicate with somebody working in that position and ask him or her about qualifications and requirements.
- Contact an agency that hires that position and ask about qualifications and requirements.
- Check with your high school counselor.
- Ask the reference department at your public library.
- Write to a related association or organization (see Appendix A and Appendix B).
- Contact the NASW (see Appendix A).

Schools

A number of resources are available to help you explore what type of educational programs are available at vocational schools, community colleges, and state and private universities. Contact your high school guidance counselor, your public library, or the schools themselves.

High School Counselor

Your high school counselor should have material and information about many schools and different programs. If the counselor does not have material on a school that you are interested in, he or she should know how to contact the school and get that information.

Public Library

Libraries have volumes of information on schools, programs, and related information. Explain to the librarian what type of information you need. He or she may be able to help you find it or show you where to look. If the library doesn't have what you need, the librarian may be able to request it from another source or explain to you how to obtain it.

Two books available at some libraries will help you gather information and evaluate different programs: *The College Blue Book* by Macmillan Publishing Company, and *Peterson's Annual Guides* (series on schools) by Peterson Guides, Inc. If you are trying to decide between a number of schools, write to them all or contact them through the Internet at their individual websites. Request their catalog or school bulletin. You may want to request information on their financial aid packages at this time, too. You can compare their programs for what best fits your needs.

Accredited Programs

The Council on Social Work Education is responsible for accrediting schools in social work programs. You can write and ask the council for its list of publications at:

Council on Social Work Education
1725 Duke Street, Suite 500
Alexandria, VA 22314

Financial Aid

There are a number of student aid programs that may help you financially should you need further education to fulfill your career plans. To get more information on these and other sources of aid, contact your high school counselor, the financial aid office at the college, and/or your state scholarship agency.

A College Board publication, *Meeting College Costs*, explains how to apply for student financial aid. High school students should ask their guidance counselor for the current edition. For a list of other College Board publications, write to:

College Board Publications
45 Columbus Avenue
New York, NY 10023

For more details on federal student financial aid, write for a free copy of the booklet *The Student Guide: Financial Aid.* Ask for this booklet from:

Federal Student Aid Information Center
P.O. Box 84
Washington, DC 20044-0084

Approximately eighty-three hundred colleges, universities, and vocational and technical schools take part in the following federal financial aid programs.

Financial Programs

There are many different types of financial aid. Grants are usually an award based on financial need. A scholarship usually refers to award-based or academic merit. You are not required to pay back either of these. More than 80 percent of all aid awarded comes from federal and state needs-based programs. Contact the Federal Student Aid Information Center for any questions about federal aid programs. Call (800) 433-3243 between 9:00 A.M. and 5:30 P.M, EST.

College Work-Study

Part of your financial package may include a work-study program. College work-study jobs let you earn money to put toward your school expenses. These jobs are for both undergraduate and graduate students. Usually you have to be going to school at least half time. Some schools do award a few college work-study jobs to students who attend less than half time.

Federal Perkins Loans

Federal Perkins Loans ($4,000 for undergraduates, $6,000 for graduate students, according to *The Student Guide: Financial Aid, 2002–03*) are low-interest loans made through your school's financial aid office. You must repay this money. These loans are for both undergraduate and graduate students. Loan amounts are based on financial need and money available at the school you attend. No interest is charged while you are a student, but you must start repaying the loan nine months after you leave school at a 5 percent rate.

Subsidized and Unsubsidized Loans

The student or parents may apply for other loans ($2,625 to $18,500, depending on grade level). Obtaining subsidized loans by the government means that you don't pay interest while you are a student. In unsubsidized loans, the borrower is responsible for the interest during all periods of the loan.

With the high cost of education today, look into as many sources of aid as possible. *The Student Guide* suggests some other sources for financial aid:

- Contact the financial aid administrator at each school you are interested in attending. He or she can tell you what aid programs are available and the total cost of attending the school.

- If you are in high school, talk to your guidance counselor.
- Your public library has information on state and private sources of aid. Your financial need is usually considered for such aid, but other factors may also be considered.
- Many companies, as well as labor unions, have programs to help pay for the cost of postsecondary education for employees or members (or for their children).
- Check foundations, religious organizations, fraternities or sororities, and town or city clubs. Include community organizations and civic groups such as the American Legion, YMCA, 4-H Clubs, Kiwanis, Jaycees, Chamber of Commerce, and Girl or Boy Scouts.
- National Merit Scholarships and scholarships from the National Honor Society are available to qualifying students with high grades.
- Look into organizations connected with your field of interest.
- If you are a veteran, see if you are eligible for veteran benefits. Contact your local Veterans Administration office.
- Contact your home state's student assistance agency for information about state aid.

Your Decision

The ideal job you picture yourself in now may *not* be exactly what you end up doing. There are certain things that should affect your decision. You don't want to stumble onto a job or just end up in a career. To be happy with your career choice, you must first know your options. Then you must be honest in evaluating your abilities, interests, and needs. And once you start preparing yourself for your career by studying and through experiences, you have to keep on evaluating yourself and be willing to make a change in the direction that you are going—if necessary.

Social work is a demanding field. It is an involving field. People don't go into social work for the money, for the prestige, or for the enjoyment. Usually a person enters social work because of a need or desire to help people, to change something, or to make a difference.

Social workers are involved in social issues and social problems. There are stigmas attached to the field. And there are harsh realities. You see a side of society that many people don't even know exists. You see hurt, disappointment, sickness, desperation, depression, frustration, poverty, abuse, and strife. You see families breaking up, kids getting into trouble, and people not wanting to face realities.

You won't just be reading about these problems. You will be right in the middle of them. You have to want to work in this field. You have to want to make a difference—and you can. You may not be able to change major policies, end world hunger, or do away with abuse. But you may be able to help people learn to deal with their problems and do something with their lives. You also may help affect policy changes. You won't have all the solutions to all of the problems, but you can offer some guidance, directions, and resources. You can make a difference!

7

LOCATING A JOB

ASK YOURSELF THE following questions: Have you evaluated your skills, abilities, needs, and interests? Learned as much as you can about the job you want? Compared your skills, interests, needs, and abilities with the job? Found out if you are eligible for the position in your state or that setting? Obtained the training or education needed? If you've answered "yes" to those questions, then you are ready to start looking for employment as a social worker.

Job Skills and Job Duties

Previous work experience, volunteer positions, or internships may not have had the same title as the job you are applying for now, but the duties and roles you experienced may be similar. As you complete a résumé or application, think of your past and current jobs or related work experience as made up of skill components. You can do this for paraprofessional or preprofessional positions, too. Your potential employer isn't as concerned about what settings you have worked in as much as what experiences and skills you will be bringing to the job.

Most social work and related positions will include these skill areas:

- observation
- one-on-one counseling
- record keeping
- group counseling or group work
- interviewing
- client relationships
- team work/staff relationships
- intervention
- time/cost accountability
- appointment scheduling
- evaluations and assessments
- service coding/accountability
- networking services with professionals/agencies
- case management
- case consultations
- supervision

Consequently these are the duties and skills that you should concentrate on improving. They are also some of the duties and skill areas you should be able to include on a résumé or application.

For example, merely telling a potential employer that you worked in an adult day care center in field experience says little about what you actually did (especially if the employer doesn't actually know what adult day care is). Explain that you:

- observed and maintained relationships with elderly clients
- kept daily records on their activities and your observations

- interviewed potential new clients and their families
- worked as a team member in providing supportive services
- took part in evaluations and assessments
- coordinated resources with other agencies
- produced written reports
- set up and coordinated group activities
- consulted with other professionals

These are the types of duties or responsibilities that make up a job description.

Even if the setting or previous experience is totally different from the job you want, you probably do have experience in some of the duties or skill areas. Break down your other work experiences, especially those related to social work, into duties. Compare those with a detailed job description of the job you want. Accentuate similar skills/job duties when interviewing for a job. In other words, look for similarities—not differences—between your work experience and the job you want.

Once you have accomplished that, you are ready to start applying for appropriate jobs. But since you may not be able to contact all the open positions in person, you need to prepare a paper that will introduce you and who you are.

The Résumé

A résumé is a written statement that you want to give or send to employers. This paper will represent you for the job you are applying for. It tells the employer who you are, what you know, and what you have done. It is your initial contact with an employer. You want to represent yourself well in hopes that the employer will become interested enough to offer you an interview.

A résumé does three things. First, it helps you contact more employers than you could personally visit. Second, it makes you think about your qualifications, organize them, and put them in writing. And third, it serves as a visual reminder of you to the employer after your interview.

To prepare a résumé, first gather all the material, facts, and information that represent your work history, education, and personal qualifications. Select and organize this material in a way that will best represent you. On the top of the page list your name, address, phone number, and E-mail address (if applicable). Then under the heading "Employment Objectives," list the specific job you are interested in.

If you have a related work history, then briefly describe jobs under the heading "Work Experience." Remember to stress responsibilities and duties that may apply to the position you are interested in. You may separate this section into the specific jobs and the dates that you were employed in different settings. Or you may organize your work experience into categories of responsibilities and duties—for example, interviewing, assessment and evaluation, record keeping, supervision, and group work. Then describe the duties and responsibilities you have had in these areas.

Then add "Education." If you lack work experience and education is your strong point, list "Education" before "Work Experience." You may include a final section, "Miscellaneous." Here you highlight other important information, such as computer skills, knowledge of a foreign language, volunteer or leisure time experiences, membership in professional organizations, or other related accomplishments or skills.

When you send out your résumé, be sure to include a cover letter. This letter of application asks for an interview. In this one-page letter you should:

- Explain how you heard of the opening or potential opening.
- State exactly what position you are applying for and why you are interested in the particular firm.
- Refer to your attached résumé and ask for an interview to discuss your application in more detail.

Proofread your résumé and cover letter very carefully after it has been typed. Use the spell check feature on your computer to catch all possible errors. *Never* mail a résumé to a potential employer with spelling or grammatical errors. Remember that you want to make a good impression!

Sample Résumé

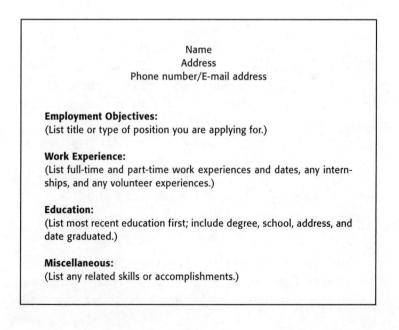

Name
Address
Phone number/E-mail address

Employment Objectives:
(List title or type of position you are applying for.)

Work Experience:
(List full-time and part-time work experiences and dates, any internships, and any volunteer experiences.)

Education:
(List most recent education first; include degree, school, address, and date graduated.)

Miscellaneous:
(List any related skills or accomplishments.)

State and Federal Government Positions

Individuals interested in working for state or local agencies should contact the appropriate agencies. City, county, and state personnel and human resources departments, and local offices of state employment services have applications and additional information. Other information about careers in government is available from:

U.S. Employment Service
200 Constitution Avenue NW
Washington, DC 20212

The Council of State Governments
P.O. Box 11910
Lexington, KY 40578-1910
csg.org

Specific information on obtaining a position with the federal government is available from the Office of Personnel Management (OPM) through a telephone-based system. Consult your telephone directory under "U.S. Government" for a local number or call (912) 757-3000. Information is also available from the OPM Internet website: usajobs.opm.gov.

Information on many occupations commonly employed by local, state, and federal government may be found in the *Occupational Outlook Handbook*. This book is published annually by the government and is available at all public and academic libraries. You can also view this book online at bls.gov/oco.

Civil Service

The U.S. Civil Service Commission handles U.S. government civilian jobs. Jobs are located throughout the United States and overseas. These jobs are filled on a merit basis as determined by examinations and rating of experience and education. Examinations are given several times a year. Tests for entry-level professional positions are conducted at many universities and other schools. Most post offices have forms and information on job opportunities.

Getting on a list doesn't guarantee staying on the list or getting a job. When job openings develop, some names of candidates are given to the employer by this testing system. The employer then has a number of people to interview for perhaps only one position. Be sure to ask how long you stay on this list and when you need to reapply. On state lists you may have to indicate what part of the state you would be willing to work in. Federal lists may also ask you to indicate regions or parts of the country where you would be willing to work.

Additional Job Leads

Besides government and civil service openings, many other sources have information about jobs. Talk to or check with:

- state employment services
- school or college placement services
- want ads in newspapers and professional journals
- association registries
- relatives or friends, social or business contacts
- industrial and craft unions
- yellow pages of the telephone directory

For other social work positions in local, municipal, private, or community centers or programs such as nursing homes, hospitals, mental health centers, chemical dependency treatment programs, neighborhood centers, prevention programs, industry, or schools and community action programs, apply at their local agencies through the personnel office. If you need to be on any registry or list, they will tell you. If you are only interested in local positions, consult the yellow pages in the phone book and send out résumés or call and talk to potential employers.

Before mailing out applications, call the agency and talk to the personnel department or whoever takes applications. Ask the individual if he or she is taking applications or if applications are kept on file. Inquire about any special qualifications needed for the job you are interested in and if the agency is expecting any openings in the near future. If you are especially interested in a particular agency, try to arrange an informal interview to fill out its application form. This meeting will help acquaint you with the agency and establish an inside contact person.

The Interview

Although your qualifications and education are important, the employer's first impression of you may make the difference in whether you get the job. Make the best impact you can by following these recommendations:

- Be at least ten minutes early for the appointment.
- Bring a copy of your résumé. Also have other personal data prepared and organized to help you fill out the firm's job application.
- Let the interviewer lead the discussion and look the interviewer in the eye while you are talking.

- Answer questions by stressing your training, experience, skill, and accomplishments that qualify you for the job.
- Answer questions truthfully. Do not criticize former employers or coworkers.
- Avoid negative responses. Find a way to turn a negative into a positive response.
- If possible, find out ahead of time about the salary range for this type of job.
- When the interviewer asks if you have any questions, don't concentrate on salary. Ask about advancement, about the agency, or other questions about the job.
- At the end of the interview, thank the interviewer for his or her time. Let the interviewer know if you want the job.
- If you are sincerely interested in the position, send a follow-up letter. Thank the interviewer again for his or her time and express an interest in the job.

8

Social Work Opportunities in Canada

As in the United States, the majority of jobs for social workers in Canada are funded directly or indirectly by the municipal, provincial, or federal governments. Others work for agencies funded by voluntary donations. Settings for social workers may be found at:

- family and child welfare agencies
- hospitals and other health care facilities
- group homes and hostels
- addiction treatment facilities
- social assistance offices
- settlement houses
- community centers
- grassroots social action organizations

- government offices
- social planning councils

A small yet growing number of social workers, however, is self-employed. Social workers may either offer services to the public for fees or contract services to large organizations. Salaries of social workers vary from province to province.

Canadian Association of Schools of Social Work

The Canadian Association of Schools of Social Work (CASSW) is the national body that accredits schools and departments of social work. The CASSW is the Canadian equivalent to the United States' Council on Social Work Education (CSWE). Since 1967 the CASSW has been a voluntary association of university faculties, schools, and departments offering professional education in social work at the undergraduate, graduate, and postgraduate levels. CASSW replaced the National Committee of Schools of Social Work.

According to the CASSW mission statement, which was approved by the General Assembly on June 15, 1994, it fulfills its purpose through: development of educational policies and standards; accreditation of social work education programs; conduct of research and the promotion of scholarly activity; dissemination of information through publications and annual conferences; and provision of critical analyses and public comment on issues affecting the education of social workers and the nature of social welfare policies and services.

Education and Training

In most provinces the B.S.W. (Bachelor of Social Work) is the minimum educational requirement for entry in the social work profession. An additional year is needed for the M.S.W. (Master of Science) degree if you already have a B.S.W. If you have a nonsocial work degree, a two-year program is necessary. A doctorate degree is needed for those who want to teach at a university or for involvement in research, social policy, or large-scale administration. The CASSW has a directory that explains the different programs offered in each of these universities. To contact the CASSW, write to:

Canadian Association of Schools of Social Work
383 Parkdale Avenue, Suite 206
Ottawa, ON K1Y 4R4
Canada
(613) 792-1953
cassw-acess.ca

Canadian Association of Social Workers

The Canadian Association of Social Workers (CASW) is the Canadian equivalent to the United States' National Association of Social Workers (NASW). It was founded in 1926 to monitor employment conditions and to establish standards of practice within the profession and evolved into a national voice on behalf of approximately fifteen thousand members. Social workers automatically become affiliated with the CASW when they join the appropriate provincial association. (See Appendix B for a list of provincial associations and affiliate organizations.) Because of this broad-based membership, they are able to offer benefits and advantages such as insurance packages that include professional liability insurance, group life, disability, and a retirement plan.

On a national level, CASW takes a pro-active approach to issues pertinent to social work. It produces for its members materials on such critical issues as poverty, unemployment, multiculturalism, and domestic violence. It also acts as a clearinghouse for its member organizations, providing information related to social work policy and practice. The code of ethics, national policy and position papers, research projects, reports, and selected books are also available from the national office. The CASW also publishes *Canadian Social Work*, a national professional journal. It is published in both English and French versions, per subscriber request (see Appendix C for more information).

To contact CASW, write:

Canadian Association of Social Workers
383 Parkdale Avenue, Suite 402
Ottawa, ON K1Y 4R4
Canada
(613) 729-6668
casw-acts.ca

Certification/Registration

Contact individual provinces for specific certification and registration information. The following are addresses (including available websites, CASW update 2001: casw-acts.ca) for the Canadian

Registrars for Certification in each province. See also Appendix B for additional Canadian organizations.

Alberta
Alberta College of Social Workers
#550 10707 100 Ave.
Edmonton, AB T5J 3M1
Canada
(780) 421-1167
acsw.ab.ca
Executive Director, Registrar, Rod Adachi

British Columbia
Board of Registration for Social Workers of British
  Columbia
#407-1755 W. Broadway
Vancouver, BC V6J 4S5
Canada
(604) 737-4916
brsw.bc.ca
Registrar, Susan Irwin

Manitoba
Manitoba Association of Social Workers/Manitoba
  Institute of Registered Social Workers
Unit 4-2015 Av Portage Ave.
Winnepeg, MB R3J 0K3
Canada
(204) 888-9477
geocities.com/MASW-MIRSW
Executive Director, Registrar, Miriam Browne

New Brunswick
New Brunswick Association of Social Workers
P.O. Box 1533, Station A
Fredericton, NB E3B 5G2
Canada
(506) 459-5595
nbasw-atsnb.ca
Executive Director, Registrar, Suzanne McKenna

Newfoundland
Newfoundland & Labrador Association of Social Workers
P.O. Box 5244, East End Post Office
St. John, NF A1C 5W1
Canada
(709) 753-0200
www3.nf.sympatico.ca/n/asw
Executive Director, Registrar, Patricia Erving

Nova Scotia
Nova Scotia Association of Social Workers
1891 rue Brunswick
Halifax, NS B3J 2G8
Canada
(902) 429-7799
nsasw.org
Executive Director, Harold Beals
Registrar, Brenda Richard

Ontario
Ontario College of Social Workers and Social Service Workers
80 Bloor St. W., Ste. 401
Toronto, ON M5S 2V1
Canada
(416) 972-9882
ocswssw.org
Registrar, Glenda McDonald

Prince Edward Island
Prince Edward Island Social Work Registration Board
81 Prince St.
Charlottetown, PE C1A 4R3
Canada
(902) 368-7337

Quebec
Ordre professionnel des travailleurs sociaux du Quebec
5757 Ave. Decelles, Bureau 335
Montreal, PQ H3S 2C3
Canada
(514) 731-3925
Registrar, Rene Page

Saskatchewan
Saskatchewan Association of Social Workers
2110 Lorne St.
Regina, SK S4P 2M5
Canada
(306) 545-1922
Registrar, Rawd Bieber

9

RELATED OCCUPATIONS

SOCIAL WORKERS HELP people solve personal problems through direct counseling, referrals, and other services. They are also employed in almost every type of setting where people work with people.

In each of these settings there are related professionals who do similar or supportive work. Just as social workers deal with people and their environment, other professionals work with people in other specializations. The Department of Labor's *Occupational Outlook Handbook* has employment facts and information about the duties of many of these similar professionals. Some of these affiliated careers are:

- psychologists (clinical, counseling, school, industrial, community, health)
- counselors (guidance, rehabilitation, employment, mental health)
- social and human service assistants
- clergy

Psychologists

Psychologists study human behavior and mental processes to help them understand and explain people's actions. Their duties and responsibilities also vary depending on their training and setting.

Clinical psychologists generally work in hospitals, clinics, or private practices. They help the mentally or emotionally disturbed adjust to life. They interview patients, give diagnostic tests, provide psychotherapy, and design behavior-modification programs.

Counseling psychologists use several techniques, including interviewing and testing, to advise people on how to deal with personal, social, educational, or vocational problems.

School psychologists work with parents and teachers to evaluate and resolve students' learning and behavior problems.

Industrial and organizational psychologists apply psychological techniques to personnel administration, management, and marketing problems. They are involved in, among other activities, policy planning, worker training and development, psychological test research, counseling, and organizational development and analysis.

Community psychologists apply psychological knowledge to problems of urban and rural life.

Health psychologists counsel the public in health maintenance to help people avoid serious emotional or physical illness.

Working Conditions

Working conditions will depend upon the work setting. Clinical and counseling psychologists in private practice have pleasant offices and set their own hours, but they do have to accommodate clients and work some evenings. Psychologists in health facilities often work evenings and weekends. Those in schools and clinics work regular hours. Work in government and industry may mean more structured hours, working alone at desks with research materials and writing reports. They may experience the pressures of deadlines, tight schedules, heavy workloads, and overtime work.

Employment

Psychologists held approximately 182,000 jobs in 2000. Educational institutions employed about 40 percent of all salaried psychologists in positions involving counseling, testing, special education, research, and administration. Three out of ten psychologists are employed in hospitals, clinics, rehabilitation centers, nursing homes, and other health facilities. One out of ten psychologists are employed by the government at the federal, state, and local levels.

The Veterans Administration, the Department of Defense, and the Public Health Service employ more psychologists than other federal agencies. Other positions are found in social service organizations, research organizations, management consulting firms, market research firms, and other businesses. More than one-fourth of all psychologists are self-employed.

Training, Qualifications, and Advancement

A doctorate degree is usually required for employment as a psychologist in academic positions. People with a master's degree in psychology can administer and interpret tests as psychological assistants. They may teach in a two-year college or work as school psychologists or counselors. People with a bachelor's degree can assist psychologists and other professionals in mental health centers, vocational rehabilitation offices, and correctional programs.

They may also work as research or administrative assistants. There is little chance that people with bachelor's degrees will advance unless they have more education.

People entering psychology must be emotionally stable, mature, and able to deal effectively with people. For clinical work and counseling, the ability to lead and inspire others and be sensitive and compassionate are important.

Job Outlook and Earnings

Employment of psychologists is expected to increase faster than average for all occupations through 2010. Increased emphasis on health maintenance rather than treatment, public concern for the development of human resources, the growing elderly population, and increased testing and counseling of children are all factors involved in maintaining the demand for psychologists.

Average annual earnings of salaried psychologists were $48,596 in 2002. Median earnings for clinical, counseling, and school psychologists were $48,320. Industrial-organizational psychologists earned $66,800 annually.

The federal government starts psychologists with a bachelor's degree at about $21,900, and those with superior academic records could begin at $27,200. Counseling psychologists with a master's degree and one year of counseling experience could start at $33,300. The average salary for psychologists in the federal government was about $72,830 in 2001.

Additional Information

For additional information on careers, educational requirements, licensing, and financial assistance, contact:

American Psychological Association
750 First Street NE
Washington, D.C. 20002-4242
apa.org

Counselors

Counselors help people deal with personal, social, educational, and career problems and concerns. Like social workers, what they do depends upon their training and the setting in which they work.

Guidance or school counselors help students evaluate their abilities, interests, talents, and personality characteristics in terms of realistic academic and career options. They may use tests to help students better understand themselves. They also maintain information on college admission requirements, entrance exams, and financial aid as well as other job-training information. Counselors help students with social, behavioral, and personal problems.

Rehabilitation counselors help physically, mentally, emotionally, or socially handicapped individuals to become self-sufficient and productive citizens. They evaluate clients' employment possibilities and arrange for medical care, rehabilitation programs, occupational training, and job placement.

Employment counselors help individuals make career decisions by exploring their clients' education, training, work history, interests, skills, personal traits, and physical capacities. They may arrange for aptitude and achievement tests. They may refer clients to employers. They may also work with clients on appropriate ways to apply for jobs and write résumés, and coach them on interviewing techniques.

Mental health counselors help individuals with social and personal problems, such as substance abuse, family conflicts, physical abuse, suicide, work problems, criminal behavior, and problems of aging. They counsel rape victims, individuals trying to cope with illness and death, and people with emotional problems.

Working Conditions

Generally counselors work a forty-hour week. Self-employed and mental health counselors may have to work evenings to meet with working clients. School counselors may have a ten-, ten-and-a-half-, or eleven-month contract. Because of the need for privacy, the counselor usually has a private office.

Employment

Counselors held 465,000 jobs in 2000. Nearly two-thirds of these jobs were in education services. Most of them were in secondary schools. Rehabilitation counselors worked in state and local rehabilitation agencies, hospitals, and Veterans Administration programs. Counselors also worked in similar mental health and social service agencies that employ social workers. A growing number of counselors are in private practice, health maintenance organizations, and group practice.

Training, Qualifications, and Advancement

Generally a master's degree is required in counseling careers, but there are some entry-level jobs that consider bachelor's degrees. A one- or two-year program is usually required for a master's. Most states require public school counselors to have both counseling and teaching certificates. Mental health counselors usually have a master's degree or doctorate in mental health counseling or a related area.

School counselors may advance in their careers by moving to a larger school, becoming directors or supervisors of counseling, or going on to become an educational psychologist, vocational psychologist, school psychologist, or school administrator. In most cases, an educational or vocational psychologist must have a doctorate degree.

Other counselors may advance by going to supervisory or administrative jobs in their agency. Some go into research, consulting work, or college teaching. Others go into private practice. Thirty-two states require that counselors in private practice have a state license.

Job Outlook and Earnings

Overall employment of counselors is expected to grow about as fast as average for all occupations through 2010. In addition, replacement needs will increase significantly by the end of the decade as many counselors now in their forties reach retirement age. According to a recent survey, the average salary of school counselors in the 2000 academic year was about $42,110. Salaries vary for location and setting. Salaries of rehabilitation, mental health, and employment counselors are usually somewhat lower than are those of school counselors.

Additional Information

For more information on the general field of counseling, write to:

American Counseling Association
5999 Stevenson Avenue
Alexandria, VA 22304
counseling.org

Social and Human Service Assistants

Social and human service assistant is a term used to describe people with various job titles, including human service worker, case management aide, social work assistant, mental health aide, community support worker, community outreach worker, life skill counselor, or gerontology aide. They usually work under the direction of professionals from a variety of fields, such as nursing, psychiatry, psychology, rehabilitative therapy or physical therapy, or social work.

They provide direct and indirect client services. Social and human service assistants assess clients' needs, establish their eligibility for benefits and services, and help them obtain those services.

Working Conditions

Some social and human service assistants work in offices, clinics, and hospitals, while others work in group homes, shelters, sheltered workshops, and day programs. Many spend their time in the field visiting clients. Most work a forty-hour week; some work in the evenings and on weekends.

Employment

Social and human service assistants held approximately 271,000 jobs in 2000. About 50 percent worked in private social or human services agencies, offering a variety of services, including adult day care, group meals, crisis intervention, counseling, and job training. Many supervise residents of group homes and halfway houses. About one-fourth were employed by the state and local governments, mostly in public welfare agencies and facilities for the mentally disabled and developmentally challenged.

Training, Qualifications, and Advancement

A bachelor's degree usually is not required for entry into this occupation; however, employers look for individuals with relevant work experience or education beyond high school. Certificates or associate degrees in subjects such as human services, social work, gerontology, or one of the social or behavioral sciences will meet most employers' requirements. Employers select applicants who have effective communication skills, the ability to manage time effectively, and a strong sense of responsibility.

Formal education almost always is necessary for advancement. In general, advancement requires a bachelor's or master's degree in rehabilitation, counseling, human services, social work, psychology, or a related field.

Job Outlook and Earnings

Overall employment for social and human service assistants is expected to be very good, especially for applicants with postsecondary education. The number of social and human service assistants is projected to grow much faster than the average for all occupations through 2010.

According to U.S. Department of Labor statistics, annual earnings of social and human service assistants were $22,330 in 2000. Median annual salaries in the industries employing the largest numbers of social and human service assistants in 2000 were: state government (excluding education and hospitals), $27,130; local governments (excluding education and hospitals), $25,320; social services, $21,820; individual and family services, $21,350; and resident care, $19,880.

Additional Information

Information on academic programs in human services may be found in most directories of two- and four-year colleges and are available at libraries or career counseling centers.

For further information on careers and programs in human services, write to:

National Organization for Human Service Education
University of Rhode Island
Quinn 107-URI
Kingston, RI 02881

Employment information may be available from state employment service offices or directly from city, county, or state departments of health, mental health, and human services.

Clergy

The duties and responsibilities of the clergy differ depending upon denomination and the size of the congregation. They may lead their congregations in worship services and administer rites of baptism, confirmation, and Holy Communion. They prepare sermons and give religious instruction. They may perform marriages, conduct funerals, counsel individuals, and visit the sick, aged, and handicapped at home and in the hospital.

Working Conditions

Ministers are on call for any serious trouble or emergencies that affect the members of the congregation. They also may work long and irregular hours in administrative, educational, and community services. Many duties are sedentary, as they do research, prepare sermons, or read. In some denominations the clergy are expected to move to another parish every few years.

Employment

The majority of clergy serve as religious leaders in communities of any size—major metropolitan through sparsely rural areas—throughout the nation. Other members of the clergy serve their religious communities in ways that do not call for them to hold positions in congregations. Some serve as chaplains in the U.S. Armed Forces and in hospitals, while others help to carry out the missions of religious community and social services agencies. A few members of the clergy serve in administrative or teaching posts in schools at all grade levels, including seminaries.

Training, Qualifications, and Advancement

Educational requirements for entry into the clergy vary. Similar to other professional occupations, about three out of four members of the clergy have completed at least a bachelor's degree. Many denominations require that clergy complete a bachelor's degree and a graduate-level program of theological study. Individuals considering careers in the clergy should consult their religious leaders to verify specific entrance requirements.

Religious leaders must exude confidence and motivation, while remaining tolerant and able to listen to the needs of others. They should be capable of making difficult decisions, working under pressure, and living up to the moral standards set by their faith and community.

Job Outlook and Earnings

Rising costs and inadequate financial support due to the anticipated slow growth in church membership are expected to result in only limited growth in the need for ministers through 2010. Jobs for rabbis are favorable, especially in nonmetropolitan areas, where more priests will also be needed. Alternatives for newly ordained ministers could be to work in youth counseling, family relations, and welfare organizations; teach in religious educational institutions; and serve as chaplains in the armed forces, hospitals, universities, and correctional institutions.

Salary is usually not a factor in influencing a person's decision whether to enter the field. Most people in the clergy feel they have a calling to serve. Some clergy have to take outside employment to make ends meet, especially those who have families.

Additional Information

People interested in the clergy should talk to members of their religious community. Their religious leaders should be able to help them evaluate their qualifications and give them more information on educational requirements.

Appendix A

National Associations and Organizations

FOLLOWING ARE ASSOCIATIONS and organizations to contact for more information.

Social Work Organizations

American Association of State Social Work Boards
400 S. Ridge Pkwy., Ste. B
Culpeper, VA 22701

American Public Human Services Association
801 First St. NE, Ste. 500
Washington, DC 20002

Clinical Social Work Federation
P.O. Box 3740
Arlington, VA 22203

Council on Social Work Education
1725 Duke St., Ste. 500
Alexandria, VA 22314

National Association of Black Social Workers
8436 W. McNichols Ave.
Detroit, MI 48221

National Association of Social Workers
750 First St. NE, Ste. 700
Washington, DC 20002

North American Association of Christians in Social Work
P.O. Box 121
Botsford, CT 06404

Supportive Organizations

Alcohol and Drug Problems Association of North America
307 N. Main St.
St. Charles, MO 63301

American Association of Homes and Services for the Aging
2519 Connecticut Ave. NW
Washington, DC 20008

American Association for International Aging
1900 L St. NW, Ste. 510
Washington, DC 20036

American Humane Association, Children's Services
63 Inverness Dr.
Englewood, CO 80112

Catholic Charities USA
1731 King St., Ste. 200
Alexandria, VA 22314

Child Welfare League of America
440 First St. NW, Ste. 310
Washington, DC 20001

Children's Defense Fund
25 E St. NW
Washington, DC 20001

Children's Foundation
725 Fifteenth St. NW, Ste. 505
Washington, DC 20005

Coalition for Economic Survival
1296 N. Fairfax Ave.
Los Angeles, CA 90046

National Center for Missing and Exploited Children
747 Third Ave., 16th Fl.
New York, NY 10017

National Clearinghouse on Child Abuse and Neglect Information
330 C St. SW
Washington, DC 20447

National Committee for the Prevention of Elder Abuse
119 Belmont St.
Worcester, MA 01605

National Community Action Foundation
810 First St. NE, Ste. 530
Washington, DC 20002

National Council on the Aging
409 Third St. SW, Ste. 200
Washington, DC 20024

National Council on Alcoholism and Drug Dependence
20 Exchange Place, Ste. 2902
New York, NY 10005

National Council of Senior Citizens
8403 Colesville Rd., Ste. 1200
Silver Spring, MD 20910

National Crime Prevention Council
1000 Connecticut Ave. NW
Washington, DC 20036

National Urban League
120 Wall St.
New York, NY 10005

Prevent Child Abuse
200 S. Michigan Ave.
Chicago, IL 60604

Volunteers of America
1660 Duke St.
Alexandria, VA 22314

APPENDIX B

Canadian Associations

FOLLOWING ARE CANADIAN associations and organizations to contact for more information.

Social Work Associations

Alberta Association of Social Workers
#52, 10707 100 Ave. NW
Edmonton, AB T5J 3M1
Canada

The Association of Social Workers of Northern Canada
Box 600
Fort Smith, NWT, X0E 0P0
Canada

British Columbia Association of Social Workers
Suite 402
1755 W. Broadway Ouest
Vancouver, BC (C-B) V6J 4S5
Canada

Canadian Association of Social Workers
383 Parkdale Ave., Ste. 402
Ottawa, ON K1Y 4R4
Canada

Manitoba Association of Social Workers/Manitoba Institute of
    Registered Social Workers
Unit 4—2015 Av Portage Ave.
Winnipeg, MN R3J OK3
Canada

New Brunswick Association of Social Workers
P.O. Box CP 1533
Postal Station/Succersale A
Fredericton, NB (N-B) E3B 5G2
Canada

Newfoundland and Labrador Association of Social Workers
P.O. Box/CP 5244
East End Post Office/Succersale de l'Est
St. John's, NF (T-N) A1C 5W1
Canada

Nova Scotia Association of Social Workers
1891 rue Brunswick St., Ste./Bureau 106
Halifax, NS (N-E) B3J 2G8
Canada

Ontario Association of Social Workers
410 rue Jarvis St.
Toronto, ON M4Y 2G6
Canada

Ordre professionel des travailleurs sociaux du Québec
5757 ave. Décelles, Bureau 335
Montréal (PQ) H3S 2C3
Canada

Prince Edward Island Association of Social Workers
81 rue Prince St.
Charlottetown, PE (I-P-é) C1A 4R3
Canada

Saskatchewan Association of Social Workers
2110 Lorne St.
Regina, SK S4P 2M5
Canada

Affiliate Organizations

Canadian Coalition for the Rights of Children
327-180 Argyle Ave.
Ottawa, ON K2P 1B7
Canada

Canadian Nurses Association
The Health Action Lobby
50 Driveway
Ottawa, ON K2P 1E2
Canada

Canadian Public Health Organization
1565 Carling Ave., Ste. 400
Ottawa, ON K1Z 8R1
Canada

The Coalition of National Voluntary Organizations
301-75 Albert St.
Ottawa, ON K1P 5E7
Canada

Family Service Association
22 Wellesley St. East
Toronto, ON M4Y 1G3
Canada

National Associations Active in Criminal Justice
383 Parkdale Ave., Ste. 308
Ottawa, ON K1Y 4R4
Canada

Appendix C

Journals

The periodicals listed below are good sources of information about the field of social work.

U.S. Periodicals

Administration in Social Work
Haworth Press
10 Alice St.
Binghamton, NY 13904
(800) 342-9676
getinfo@haworthpressinc.com

Child Welfare
Child Welfare League of America, Inc.
440 First St. NW
Washington, DC 20001
(202) 638-2952
journal@cwla.org

Clinical Social Work Journal
Clinical Social Work Federation
P.O. Box 3740
Arlington, VA 22203

Community Mental Health Journal
Kluwer Academic Publications
P.O. Box 358, Accord Station
Hingham, MA 02018
kluwer@wkap.com

Families in Society ·
Manticore Publishers
P.O. Box 711
Lewiston, NY 14092
(905) 845-7221
isabel@manticore.ca

Health & Social Work
NASW Press
750 First St. NE, Ste. 700
Washington, DC 20002
(202) 408-8600

Journal of Family Social Work
Haworth Press
10 Alice St.
Binghamton, NY 13904
(607) 722-5857
getinfor@haworthpressinc.com

Journal of Social Policy
Cambridge University Press, Journals Department
40 W. Twentieth St.
New York, NY 10011
(212) 924-3900

Journal of Social Work
Council on Social Work Education
1600 Duke St.
Alexandria, VA 22314
(703) 683-8080

Protecting Children
American Humane Association, Children's Division
63 Inverness Dr. East
Englewood, CO 80112
(303) 792-9900

Public Welfare
American Public Human Services Association
c/o Publication Services
810 First St. NE, Ste. 500
Washington, DC 20002
(202) 682-0100

School Social Work Journal
c/o Illinois Association School Social Workers
Box 634
Algonquin, IL 60102
(847) 676-3365

Social Policy
Union Institute
25 W. Forty-Third St., Rm. 620
New York, NY 10036
(212) 642-2929

Social Services Review
University of Chicago Press
Box 37005
Chicago, IL 60637
(773) 753-3347

Social Work
NASW/NASW Press
750 First St. NE, Ste. 700
Washington, DC 20002
(202) 408-8600

Social Work Research
NASW/NASW Press
750 First St. NE, Ste. 700
Washington, DC 20002
(202) 408-8600

Canadian Periodicals

Canadian Public Policy
University of Toronto Press
5201 Dufferin St.
North York, ON M3H 5T8
Canada
(416) 667-7810

Canadian Review of Social Policy
Carleton University
1125 Colonel Bay Dr.
Social Sciences Research Building, Rm. 304
Ottawa, ON K1S 5B6
Canada
(613) 520-7511

Canadian Social Work Review
75 University Ave. West
Waterloo, ON N2L 3C5
Canada
(519) 884-0710

Appendix D

Further Reading

FOLLOWING ARE BOOKS that cover the social work profession as well as books on searching for a job.

Social Work Profession Books

Addams, Jane. *Twenty Years at Hull House.* New York: St. Martin's Press, 1999.

Barker, Robert, and William Schroeder, eds. *The Social Work Dictionary.* Washington: NASW Press, 1999.

Block, Peter. *Stewardship: Choosing Service Over Self-Interest.* San Francisco: Berrett-Koehler Publishers, 1996.

Coles, Robert. *The Call of Service: A Witness to Idealism.* Boston: Houghton-Mifflin Co., 1994.

Colvin, Donna, and Ralph Nader, eds. *Good Works: A Guide to Careers in Social Change.* New York: Barricade Books, Inc., 1993.

Congress, Elaine P. *Social Work Values and Ethics: Identifying and Resolving Professional Dilemmas.* Chicago: Nelson-Hall, Inc., 1999.

Davies, Martin. *The Essential Social Workers: An Introduction to Professional Practice in the 1990s.* Brookfield, VT: Ashgate Publishing Co., 1994.

Doelling, Carol Nesslein. *Social Work Career Development: A Handbook for Job Hunting and Career Planning.* Washington, DC: NASW Press, 1999.

Elshtain, Jean Bethke. *Jane Addams and the Dream of American Democracy.* New York: Basic Books, 2001.

Firestone, Mary. *Social Workers.* Mankato, MN: Capstone Press, 2001.

Gil, David G. *Confronting Injustice and Oppression: Concepts and Strategies for Social Workers.* New York: Columbia University Press, 1998.

Ginsberg, Leon H. *Careers in Social Work.* Needham Heights, MA: Allyn & Bacon, Inc., 2000.

Popple, Philip, and Leslie Leighninger. *The Policy Based Profession: An Introduction to Social Welfare Policy Analysis for Social Workers.* Needham Heights, MA: Allyn & Bacon, Inc., 2000.

Richards, Keith N. *Tender Mercies: Inside the World of a Child Abuse Investigator.* Washington: Child Welfare League of America, Inc., 1999.

Saltzman, Andrea, and David M. Furman. *Law in Social Work Practice.* Chicago: Nelson-Hall, Inc., 1999.

Shore, Bill. *The Cathedral Within: Transforming Your Life by Giving Something Back.* New York: Random House, Inc., 1999.

Trattner, Walter I. *From Poor Law to Welfare State: A History of Social Welfare in America.* New York: Simon & Schuster Trade, 1999.

Wagner, David. *The Quest for a Radical Profession: Social Service Careers and Political Ideology.* Lanham, MD: University Press of America, 1990.

General Job Search Books

Adams, Bob. *The Adams Resume Almanac: 600 Resumes and 25 Cover Letters Arranged by Career Category.* Holbrook, MA: Adams Media Corp., 1994.

Bolles, Richard Nelson. *What Color Is Your Parachute, 2002.* Berkeley, CA: Ten Speed Press, 2001.

Fournier, Myra, and Jeffrey Spin. *Encyclopedia of Job-Winning Resumes: 400 Resumes.* Ridgefield, CT: Round Lake Publishing Co., 1993.

Hansen, Katharine. *Dynamic Cover Letters for New Graduates.* Berkeley, CA: Ten Speed Press, 1998.

Hawk, Barbara Spencer. *What Employers Really Want: The Insider's Guide to Getting a Job.* Lincolnwood, IL: VGM Career Books, 1998.

Kaplan, Robbie Miller, and Rosalie Maggio. *How to Say It in Your Job Search.* Upper Saddle River, NJ: Prentice Hall Press, 2001.

Mendlin, Ronald C., Marc Polonsky, et al. *Job Search Tools: Resumes, Applications, and Cover Letters.* Indianapolis: JIST Works, 2000.

Noble, David F. *Gallery of Best Cover Letters: A Collection of Quality Cover Letters by Professional Resume Writers.* Indianapolis: JIST Works, 2000.

Noble, David F. *Professional Resumes for Executives, Managers, and Other Administrators: A New Gallery of Best Resumes by Professional Resume Writers.* Indianapolis: JIST Works, 1998.

Yate, Martin John, and Martin Yate. *Cover Letters That Knock 'Em Dead.* Holbrook, MA: Adams Media Corp., 2000.

GLOSSARY

Acquired Immune Deficiency Syndrome (AIDS) A potentially life-threatening disease caused by the HIV virus, which is spread when one person comes into contact with the infected bodily fluids of another person, usually through the use of shared contaminated needles in drug use or unprotected sexual activity.

Adoption A social worker in the field of adoption does preplacement studies, places child in a home, assists with legal adoption, and does postadoption counseling and services. Searches for genetic parents.

Aftercare A support group or counseling for chemically dependent or mentally ill persons following formal treatment.

Assessment Evaluation of an individual or family's personal problems, mental or nervous disorders, chemical use, or other social, health, and behavior problems. This is done by client interviews, review of records, and testing to determine which services are needed.

Caregivers People who give direct care, such as foster parents, child care staff, or adult day care staff.

Case management Coordinating and monitoring services for people to help them meet their needs. This may include client assessment and service plans, monitoring, and evaluating clients' progress and clients' rights.

Chemotherapy Using medications to control or eliminate severe behavioral problems due to mental or emotional illnesses, or in chemical dependency treatment.

Congregate housing Shared housing arrangements for groups of older persons. Some meals and social service programs are usually provided.

Consulting services Services provided by an expert on an area or subject or services to others who cannot afford a staff person with this knowledge, such as a hospital social worker providing consultation service to nursing home staff.

Continuing care retirement community A community that provides services and housing options to meet the needs of the elderly. It provides independent and congregate living and personal, intermediate, and skilled nursing care. It strives to create an environment that allows each resident to participate in the community's life to whatever degree desired.

Contracting services Providing a service for a set fee. For example, an occupational or industrial social worker may contract with a company to provide so many hours of counseling for a certain amount of money.

Counseling services Professional help for individuals or families. Counseling services deal with problems due to personal relationships or stress.

Day care for adults Personal care and development for adults in a protective setting.

Day care for children Personal care to substitute for or supplement the child rearing provided by the child's parents.

Day treatment Structured services for individuals with mental health problems. Treatment may be devoted to teaching of living skills, rehabilitation, therapy, and social skills.

Diagnostic services Tests and evaluations needed to make a decision for the type of care or treatment.

Discharge planning Evaluation and assessment of a patient's needs starting from the day of admission. It involves looking at family, extended family, or other factors to determine what resources are available to help the patient in returning home or if plans should be made for placement elsewhere.

Disorder An abnormal physical or mental condition.

Educational assistance Education or training services that are unrelated to employment. Such services might include special education help to the blind, deaf, and others with disabilities.

Educational counseling Teaches the community about programs and concerns within that particular setting. This also includes consultation done for other agencies.

Educational/cultural services A broad educational program that enhances the problem-solving abilities, skills, and knowledge of participants.

Emergency assistance Immediate short-term assistance for individuals or families in a financial crisis.

Emergency placement Short-term residential protective setting for persons in need.

Employability services Services that help a nonhandicapped person to get, keep, or improve employment through vocational counseling, testing, job-finding skills, or vocational and college training.

Empower To give authority or power to do something.

Energy assistance Financial assistance for low-income people with high energy costs.

Family life education Presentations or workshops on marriage, parenting, and family or couple communications.

Family planning Social, educational, or medical services and supplies to help individuals determine family size or prevent unplanned pregnancies. This includes birth control counseling and referral, pregnancy testing, sterilization counseling, venereal disease referrals, public education service, and infertility counseling and referrals.

Financial counseling Helps individuals and families having financial problems to handle their finances, pay their bills, and plan for the future.

Follow-up services Interviews with a client and/or an agency to determine whether a referred client has received the service and whether the service was useful.

Food shelf Gathers food to be distributed to those in need.

Food stamps Stamps purchased for a certain amount of money and then exchanged for a larger quantity of food at grocery stores. For example, $60 worth of food stamps may be bought for only $20, but these stamps may be exchanged at the store for $60 worth of food.

Foster care services for adults Twenty-four-hour supervised living arrangements for adults in a family setting with access to social services and community resources.

Foster care services for children Twenty-four-hour substitute family or group home care for a planned period of time. This home provides experiences and conditions that promote normal growth. The child, his or her family, and the foster parents are provided with casework services and other treatment or community services.

Friendly visiting Regular visits to isolated, homebound, or institutionalized elderly to reduce their isolation and loneliness.

Gerontology graduate certificate Integrates advanced gerontological content, aging research opportunities, and multidisciplinary practicum experiences into the social work education.

Halfway house Residential living that provides a supportive environment that emphasizes emotional growth through confrontation and support. It uses community resources and provides a smooth transition from a primary treatment facility to successful independent functions in the community.

Home health service Personal care services by trained staff. These services are provided to help people remain in their own homes. Services may include helping with baths, dressing, toileting, mobility assistance, food preparation, and escort for medical care. Medical support services may also be given by qualified staff, such as checking blood pressure, changing dressings, ensuring that medications are taken, and administering certain medications.

Home management Includes chore services, such as routine housekeeping tasks, minor household repairs, shopping, lawn care, and snow shoveling; homemaking service, which provides for and teaches child care, personal care, and home management to individuals and families; housing services, which help individuals get, keep, and improve housing and modify existing housing; and money management services, which help set up workable budgets and deal with debts.

Homemaker services General household activities provided by a trained homemaker when the individual regularly responsible for these activities is temporarily absent or unable to manage the home and care for himself or herself or others in the home. Activities may include meal preparation, cleaning, simple household repairs, laundry, and shopping for food, clothing, and supplies.

Hospice care Services for people with terminal illnesses and their families. Such care provides counseling, case management, daily hygiene, and medication for the relief of pain. This is not a treatment program, but a program to allow the patient to be comfortable. This may be provided in the home or in other appropriate settings.

Individual marriage and family counseling Helps with a variety of issues, including crisis situations, family violence, incest, suicide, family conflicts, parenting skills, communications, and stress management.

Information and referral Provides information about social and human services and helps individuals make contact with resources that can best meet their needs.

Intake coordinator Assesses clients' needs and makes referrals.

Intervention Getting involved (advocating) for a client on behalf of the client. Arranging services, such as protection and counseling, because of a concern for the safety and welfare of the client.

Legal services Arrange and provide assistance to help with civil legal matters and protection of legal rights.

Long-term care facility Refers to facilities traditionally known as nursing homes. Long-term care facilities are either skilled nursing facilities (SNFs) or intermediate care facilities (ICFs), depending on the nursing and related medical care provided.

Marriage preparation Counseling for engaged couples.

Means tests The eligibility requirements for government programs. Income tests are means tests based on income. Assets tests are means tests based on personal assets.

Medicaid The federal and state medical assistance program for the aging and other groups of persons who are eligible on the basis of requirements that include means tests. Medicaid is the main source of public assistance for nursing home costs.

Medicare A federal program set up in 1965 to assist older persons with health costs. Part A is hospital insurance (HI) that covers hospital costs. Part B is supplemental medical insurance (SMI) that covers physicians' services.

Nutrition services Includes meals, other nutrition services, and socialization experiences provided in a community setting; and home-delivered meals, which are meals provided to individuals who are homebound by reason of illness, incapacity, or disability, or who are otherwise isolated.

Outpatient treatment program for the chemically dependent A treatment program for people with problems related to the use of alcohol or other drugs.

Outreach services Services designed to locate and personally contact people in a specific geographic area or in a target group and to help them learn about and get needed services.

Person in Environment (PIE) Provides social workers with a common framework to describe client problems. Social problems may be described as to their root causes.

Pregnancy counseling Help and counseling for unmarried parents and their families. Such counseling assists with decision making, foster care for the infant, the legal freeing of a child for adoption, and teaching parenting skills, and it provides updated information for genetic parents.

Preretirement counseling Involves attention to matters such as Social Security benefits, private pension plans, medical and life insurance plans, educational and training opportunities, and employment opportunities that might be available if clients desire full-time, part-time, or volunteer employment as a second career.

Probation officer Supervises adults or juveniles who have been placed on probation (instead of being sent to prison).

Protection for adults (adult protection) Determines need for protective intervention, helps correct hazardous living conditions or situations where vulnerable adults are unable to care for themselves, and investigates evidence of neglect, abuse, or exploitation.

Protection for children (child protection) Helps families recognize the cause of any problems and strengthens parental ability to provide acceptable care.

Psychosocial Relating social conditions to mental health.

Psychotherapy Treatment of mental or emotional disorders to bring about social adjustment.

Recreational/social programs Provide opportunities for enjoyment and for building relationships and contribute to social adjustment and physical well-being.

Rehabilitation Restore to a former condition or state of being.

Residential community-based care Includes board and lodging, which is supportive group living for the mentally retarded, chemically dependent, or mentally ill with minimum supervision and little or no formal program activity within the residential facility; facilities for emotionally handicapped children, which involve therapeutic care in child-caring institutions and group homes; halfway houses, which are therapeutic and supportive living arrangements for the chemically dependent and the mentally ill and that bridge the gap between residential treatment and community living; and extended care, which is very long-term care and treatment for the chemically dependent and the mentally ill with twenty-four hour supervision and almost all services provided in the facility.

Residential treatment center A family structured environment with specially trained staff. The staff members serve children who are experiencing adjustment problems in school, the community, or home and who cannot work these out while living at home. They help students grow through a variety of services. The clinical service includes individual, group, and family therapy. Support services may include psychiatric consultation, nursing services, religious development, vocational guidance, occupational and recreational therapy, and chemical abuse counseling.

Respite care Short-term care to individuals due to the absence or need for relief of those persons normally providing the care. This care may be provided during the day or overnight in the individual's home or in an out-of-home setting.

Self-determination Clients' rights to make their own choices.

Social and recreational services Arrange and provide opportunities for personal growth and development and enable individuals to participate in activities that help to maintain physical and mental vitality.

Social Security Act The federal legislation enacted in 1935. This act provides for payments to the aging, the disabled, and survivors. Major increases were enacted in 1972 and 1977.

Telephone reassurance Provides for regular telephone contacts with isolated or homebound persons to ensure continued well-being of the individual and to provide social contact.

Therapy Treatment of some type of disorder.

Title XX programs Social service programs for the aging and other needy groups that were funded until 1981 under Title XX of the Social Security Act. These programs have been converted to a more general block grant system.

Transportation services Arrange and provide travel and escort to and from community resources and facilities.

Widowed, divorced, and separated services Gives educational presentations and arranges support groups to deal with loss and provides individual grief counseling.

ABOUT THE AUTHOR

RENEE WITTENBERG is a writer and a former social worker and vocational counselor. She received her B.S. degree in social work from Bemidji State University in Minnesota. She worked as a social worker in the Redwood County Welfare and Social Service Department in Minnesota.

She also worked as a vocational counselor for the Minnesota Department of Jobs and Training. She operated her own home business as a licensed group day care provider and founded a support group for day care providers.

Renee is especially interested in coordinating social resources and services. She is the chairperson in a referral and resource committee through her church. She is on the curriculum advisory committee and is an active volunteer in the local school district.

She has written articles on children's activities and other interest areas. She has been published in such magazines as *First Teacher*, *The Inkling*, and *Let Live* and is the author of *Opportunities in Child Care Careers*, which is published by VGM Career Books.